# MAMRE

HE appeared to him at the Oaks of Mamre

Genesis

# MAMRE
## ESSAYS IN RELIGION

BY

MARTIN BUBER

TRANSLATED BY

GRETA HORT

**GREENWOOD PRESS, PUBLISHERS**
WESTPORT, CONNECTICUT

Originally published in 1946
by Melbourne University Press in association with
Oxford University Press, Melbourne and London

Reprinted from an original copy in the collections
of the Yale University Library

First Greenwood Reprinting 1970

Library of Congress Catalogue Card Number 72-97271

SBN 8371-2591-X

Printed in the United States of America

# FOREWORD

The first five of the following essays have been taken from *Kampf um Israel*, a collection of essays and lectures by Professor Buber, published in 1933 by the Schocken Verlag. The following three essays with their Foreword are a translation of *Deutung des Chassidismus*, also published by the Schocken Verlag, in 1935. The last essay has not appeared in its present form in print before. It was written in 1940 as two lectures in a series of public lectures arranged by the Hebrew University of Jerusalem. The essay gives in the main the substance of these two lectures, which were printed in the *Mosnayim*. It has been translated from Professor Buber's manuscript of the essay, which he was good enough to send me in German that I might include this important contribution to the history of Chassidism in the present volume. Though the essay deals with the rise of the chassidic movement, I have put it last in this volume, as it presupposes a knowledge of the movement as given in the preceding essays. I have with some hesitation added some notes to this volume in which I have tried to explain such terms used in the essays as may not be altogether familiar to the non-technical reader.

It is my pleasant duty to thank Dr. K. Singer and the Principal of Ormond College Theological Hall, Professor Hector Maclean for reading the translation through in manuscript. Professor Buber himself I wish to thank for the readiness with which he permitted me to publish a translation, and for his great courtesy in allowing me to publish it without submitting it to him for ratification.

GRETA HORT

*University of Melbourne*

# CONTENTS

# TRANSLATOR'S INTRODUCTION

It is a well-known fact that the English language lacks a word for the type of literature which in German is described by the word ' populär '. This linguistic paucity of the English language reflects an actual paucity ; we do not possess many men who out of their learning give the laity of their best, men who undergo the discipline and drudgery of research not primarily for the sake of the research itself, nor directly in order to become experts and specialists, but in order to communicate the best of which they are capable to the general public. If a specialist writes for the general public, his writing is incidental to .the greater part of his work, and the presumption is that it does not contain anything which merits the serious attention of other specialists ; we have ' Professoren und Pastoren ', but few ' Lehrer '. Hence the work of the Professor of Sociology in the University of Jerusalem represents a class of literature with which we are not at all familiar, and hence the difficulty of writing about it.

Looked at from the point of view of an English reader, Professor Buber's work falls into five distinct groups, which it is fairly easy to label, and a sixth group for which we have no name. The five groups consist of writings on Zionism and Chassidism ; Philosophical and Sociological Studies, Biblical Studies ; and Translation of the Bible. The sixth group consists of essays and addresses, and three slender but important volumes, all dealing with relationship : the relationship of man to God, to the world, and to his fellow-men ; or, we may say, with creation. When the subject matter of the last-named group is described in this way, it seems, however, a relatively simple matter to find a suitable name for it, for a subject like the above falls either under philosophy, more

narrowly under ethics or metaphysics, or under
theology.  But to conceive of this group as philosophical or theological would be to make a mistake
that would quickly involve us in an inability to
see what Professor Buber has given us.  Both
theology and philosophy aim at enunciating statements about their subject-matter, and, by rigorous
reasoning, arriving at closely-knit, self-contained
and self-consistent systems, be the systems theological or philosophical.  And this is just what
Professor Buber does not give us.  His interest
and his aim lie somewhere else, not in the world
as presented to and worked over by thought, but
in the world as given to man as his material for
creation ; not in God as a being about whom
certain propositions can be made and whose
existence can be grasped by bending one's mind to
follow a train of thought to its logical conclusion,
but in God as the reality whom man meets, and
to whom man can respond.  If, therefore, we
attempt to treat Professor Buber's work as being
either philosophical or theological, we immediately
find ourselves confused : we cannot reduce it to
a system, we cannot even convert what he says into
other terms in order to point out what he ' really '
means or implies, and thus compare his system
with other philosophical or theological systems.
Form and matter are inseparable in his work, a
fact which makes it particularly hazardous to
undertake a translation, for a master of style is
also a master of words, and uses words as seems
good to him, making them yield their utmost,
fitting meaning and words so closely that they
cannot be divorced, and sometimes, as I have
despairingly told myself, that they cannot be
translated.  I have therefore often been faced
with the alternative of either sacrificing meaning
to smooth English, or of retaining meaning and
sacrificing smooth English.  In all cases I have

striven to retain the meaning. Fortunately, it has usually proved to be a case of translating a phrase which is unusual in German by a phrase which is unusual in English. Thus I have translated ' Ich werde dasein, als der Ich dasein werde ' by ' I shall be there as he who I there shall be ', and thus, I hope, kept both the meaning and the arresting quality of the original phrase. In short I have attempted to follow the rules of translation given by Professor Buber himself in his book, *Die Schrift und ihre Verdeutschung.* The biblical quotations which occur throughout the essays are translated from the translation of the Bible used by Professor Buber\* ; this is the reason why they do not appear in the familiar form of the Authorised Version.

Two of Professor Buber's books have already appeared in English, *Ich und Du,* translated under the title of *I and Thou* by Ronald Gregor Smith (T. & T. Clark, 1937) and a selection of his re-telling of the legends of Baalshem translated under the title of *Jewish Mysticism and the Legends of Baalshem* by Lucy Cohen (J. M. Dent and Sons, 1931) with an essay by her on 'The Life of the Chassids '. Readers of the present book who are interested in the development of Professor Buber's thought may be referred to Hans Kohn, *Martin Buber. Sein Werk und seine Zeit* (Jakob Hegner in Hellerau, 1930, pp. 1–411), which also contains an excellent bibliography of articles and books dealing with him and his work.

What Professor Buber primarily gives us in his work is a point of view, a standing ground from which we can see and co-operate with this tremendous universe in which we are placed. Professor Buber is interested in thought in so far as it leads to action, and in action in so far as it

---

\* *Die Schrift.* Zu verdeutschen unternommen von Martin Buber gemeinsam mit Franz Rosenzweig (Lambert Schneider, 1925)

leads to the unity of God, to the unity of God with his world-indwelling glory. It is this unity which is his theme, whatever he writes about ; it is this unity he cares for above all else ; it is this unity which he recognises and describes in his works. He therefore gives neither philosophy, which shatters the unity by insisting on the dichotomy of intellect and will, of rational and non-rational ; nor theology, which reduces the unity by making God into a being about whom man thinks, and about whom the intellect alone can make true statements. The only valid name which we can give to writing such as that of Professor Buber is teaching, using the word ' teaching ' as an inadequate translation of the German word ' Lehre '. Another possible designation would be ' Way ' were it not that this word is already used in a technical sense by Taoism. Moveover, Professor Buber's teaching lays less stress on a road to be followed, on a goal to be pressed towards, than on the world-affirming, man-affirming tincture of the overflowing reality. Man is the son who recognises, and therefore rests in, his father's house, and, in doing so, makes it the home of his father and of himself. However, no one who has not experienced the change of a so-called home by the home-coming of a child ; no one who has not felt how chairs and tables, knick-knack and doors and the books on their shelves respond to the homing child will know what is meant by this. The difficulty of describing Professor Buber's teaching in any other way than by appealing to experience indicates some of the demands he makes on his readers. He does not write about religion, because what he writes is religion, and the demand he makes is that of religion. His readers, in order to grasp his thought, must be capable of recognising God ; they must, however dimly, know what is meant by the Unity.

This brings me to a question which I have asked myself many times : Is it possible for Hindu, Buddhist, Christian and Moslem readers to appreciate Professor Buber's teaching ? If these readers have a spark of religion in them, the answer is undoubtedly ' yes '. Provided that a reader is ignorant of theology and philosophy, but has a sense for reality, Professor Buber's teaching should not provide any special difficulty. If, on the other hand, the reader has a little or a great deal of theology and philosophy, the danger for him lies in the temptation to look away from the lived life in order to evaluate the teaching not by what it says or by what it does, but by its implications for some cherished intellectual conception or fervently held doctrine. One cannot read religion without being judged by religion.

This holds good about all Professor Buber's writings, for through them all runs his teaching. We can divide his work into six distinct groups, but all six groups are informed by and are manifestations of his teaching : Man as the mediator who unites God and His world-indwelling glory, and thus co-operates in the creation of the world of God.

# THE FAITH OF JUDAISM

## 1. The Way of Faith

MY subject is not the religion, but only the faith of Judaism ; I do not wish to speak to you about cultus, ritual, moral-religious standards, but only about faith, and about faith taken in its strictest and most serious sense. Not the faith to which the word ' that ' clings, not that strange, complex mingling of idle hoping and clear discerning which is denoted by the ' that ', but the faith which is construed with the preposition ' in ', the faith which implies trust and loyalty. As it is this faith which I have taken as my subject, I do not start from a Jewish theology, but from the actual attitude of believing Jews as we know it from the earliest days of Judaism down till our own time. Even though I must of necessity use theological concepts when I speak of this world of faith, I must not for a moment lose sight of the non-theological material out of which I build up this world, the literature of the people, and my own impressions of Jewish life in Eastern Europe —but there is nothing in the East of which something may not also be found in the West.

When I refer to this material, it often happens to me that some one says, ' You mean, I take it, Chassidism ?'.[1] A question which is natural enough, only it is not Chassidism which I have primarily in mind. In Chassidism I see only a movement of concentration ; it is the concretion of all those elements which are to be found in a suspended form everywhere in Judaism at all times, also in Rabbinic Judaism. Only, in Rabbinic Judaism it is not found in the visible structure of a community, but holds its sway in the hidden structure of the personal life. What I am trying to formulate may be called the theologoumena of a people's religion.

It is impossible to trace any one of these theologoumena back to any one epoch ; what is incumbent on me is to present the unity found in the changing forms. All religious truths are of a dynamic kind : They are truths which cannot be understood on the basis of a cross-section of history, but only when they are seen in the whole line of history, in their unfolding, in the dynamic of their changing forms. The most important testimony to the correctness of this view comes from the way in which these truths clarify themselves, and work themselves out to their completion ; it comes from the struggle for purity of a religious conception. The truth of the history of religion is the growing image of God, the *way* of faith. Though my subject does not impose the historical form on me, it is still of the *way* of the Jewish faith that I have to speak.

## 2. The Dialogical Situation

The question has often been raised whether a Jewish dogmatics exists or not. The emphasis should rather fall on the relative power of dogma within Judaism. That there are dogmas needs no proof in view of the incorporation of the thirteen articles of faith of Maimonides into the liturgy[2]. But dogma remains of secondary importance. In the religious life of Judaism primary importance is not given to dogma, but to the remembrance and expectation of a concrete situation : the meeting of God with men. Dogma can only arise in a situation where detachment is the prevailing attitude to the concrete, lived moment—a state of detachment which easily becomes misunderstood in dogmatics, and there comes to be regarded as superior to the lived moment. Everything which is *in abstracto*, on the thither side of the I and you confronting each other, and is thus enunciated about the divine, is only a projection on to the conceptual, constructed plane, a projection which, even while it is indispensable, proves itself again and again to be metaphorical.

It is from this point of view that we must regard the problem of so-called monotheism. Israel's experience of the ' you ' in the direct relationship, in the pure, singular experience, is so overwhelmingly strong that any notion of a plurality of principles simply cannot arise within it. Over against this stands ' the heathen ', the man who does not recognise God in his manifestations, or rather: A man is a heathen to the extent he does not recognise God in his manifestations.

The fundamental attitude of the Jews is characterised by the idea of the *jichud*, the unification, a word which has been repeatedly misunderstood. It refers to the continually renewed confirmation of the divine unity in the manifoldness of the manifestations, understood in a quite practical way. Again and again does this recognition, acknowledgement, re-finding of the divine unity happen through human vision and verification when faced by the terrific contradictions of life, and specially when faced by that *ur*-contradiction[3] which proclaims itself in multitudinous ways, and which we call the duality of good and evil. But the unification is not brought about despite these contradictions ; it is brought about in love and reconciliation ; not by merely professing the unification, but by fulfilling the profession. Therefore, the unification is not contained in any pantheistic profession, but in the reality of the impossible, in making real and actual the image, in the *imitatio Dei*. The mystery of this fact finds its completion in martyrdom, in the dying with the shout of unity on the lips, ' Hear, O Israel ',[4] which here becomes testimony in the most active way.

It is said of one of the wise men of the Middle Ages that he used to repeat, ' My God where do I find you, but where do I not find you ? ' The East-European Jewish beggar of to-day whispers softy and unfalteringly his ' Gotenju ' in the trembling and dread of his harshest hour ; the pet-name is untranslatable, naive, but in the saying of it, it becomes rich in meanings. In both there is the same recognition, the same re-acknowledgement, of the One.

It is the dialogical situation in which the human being stands that here finds its lofty or childlike expression.

Judaism regards speech as a happening which reaches out over the existence of mankind and the world. In contradiction to the static of the Logos-idea the word appears here in its full dynamic as that which comes to pass. God's act of creation is speech ; but also each lived moment is so. The world is spoken to the human beings who perceive it, and the life of man is itself a dialogue. What happens to a man are the great and small, untransmittable but unmistakable signs of his being addressed ; what he does and suffers can be an answer or a failure to answer. And thus the whole history of the world, the hidden, real world history, is a dialogue between God and his creature ; a dialogue in which man is a true, legitimate partner, who is entitled and empowered to speak his own independent word from out of his own being.

I am far from wishing to contend that the conception and experience of the dialogical situation are confined to Judaism. But I am certain that no other community of human beings have entered with such strength and fervour into this experience as have the Jews.

# 3. The Human Action

The pre-supposition for thus being in ear
with the lived dialogue, with the moment
word and answer, is, it must frankly be admitted,
that one is in earnest with the appointment of mankind to the earth.

In strongest contrast to the Iranian conception
with all its many ramifications, the Jewish conception is that the happenings in this world are
achieved not as between two principles, light and
darkness, good and evil, but between God and
men, these mortal, brittle human beings who yet
stand over against God and are able to bear his
word.

The so-called evil is then fully and as a primary
element included in the power of God, who ' forms
the light, and creates darkness '. The divine rule
is not gainsaid by anything which is evil in itself,
but by the individual human beings through whom
first the so-called evil, the directionless power, can
become real evil. Human choice is not a psycho-
logical phenomenon, but utter reality, which is
taken up into the mystery of the everlasting. It is
truly open to man to choose God or to cast him
away, and that not in a faith-relationship which is
empty of this world, but in the full content of the
everyday. The ' Fall ' did not happen once and
for all to become a fate, but in all its reality it
happens here and now. In spite of all the history
that has happened, in spite of all the inheritance
which has been bequeathed to him, each man,
woman, and child stands in the exact place of Adam,
to each is the decision given. It is true that this
does not imply that further events can be derived
from the decision ; it only implies that the choice
made by the human being is that side of reality
which concerns him as he who is called upon to
act.

Only when reality is turned into logic, when A and non-A dare not any longer dwell together, do we get determinism and indeterminism, teaching about predestination and teaching about freedom, each excluding the other. According to the logical conception of truth only one of two contraries can be true, but in the reality of the lived life they are interlocked. The individual who makes a decision knows that his deciding is no self-delusion ; the individual who has acted knows that he was and is in the hand of God. The unity of the contraries is the mystery at the innermost core of the dialogue.

I said above that evil is to be taken only as a primary element, humanly speaking as passion. Passion is only evil when it remains in the state of having no direction, when it refuses to be subject to direction, when it will not take upon itself the direction towards God—there is no other direction. In Judaism the insight recurs again and again in many forms that passion, ' the evil drive ',[5] is just the element out of which alone the great human deeds arise, also the deeds of holiness. The sentence in Scripture which says that towards the end of the last day of creation God allowed himself to judge of his work that it was ' very good ' has been taken by tradition to refer to the so-called evil drive. Of all the works of creation it is passion which is the very good, without which man cannot serve God, nor truly live. The words, ' And thou shalt love the Lord thy God with all thine heart ' are interpreted, ' With both thy drives ', with the good drive as well as with the evil drive, with the drive of direction and with the drive of strength. About this so-called evil drive does God say to man, ' You have made it evil '. Thus all ' lingering in inaction ' is the root of all evil. The act of decision implies that man does not allow himself any longer to be carried on the undirected swirl of passion, but that his whole power is joined to the direction for which he decided—and man can decide only for God.

Recently a Catholic theologian saw in this conception ' Jewish activism ' to which grace is unknown. But it is certainly not so. Man is no less in earnest with grace, because he is in earnest with the human power of deciding ; rather is it true that it is only through the latter that the soul finds the way which will lead it to the former. A plentitude of power has not in any way been given to man ; on the contrary, what has been settled for him is the perspective of the concrete action to which no bounds can be set beforehand, but which· must experience limitation and grace in the very process of acting.

The great question which is more and more deeply agitating our age is this: How can we act, is our action valid in the sight of God, or is it from its very foundation broken in pieces and unwarranted ? The question is answered as far as Judaism is concerned, because Judaism is in earnest with the conception that man has been appointed to this world as an originator of events, as a real partner in the real dialogue with God. This answer implies a refusal to have anything to do with all specific ethics, with all ethics confined to this or that sphere of life, a form of ethics which we know only too well from the spiritual history of the West. Ethics has been poured into the same mould as the religious life, and cannot be extracted from it. There is no responsibility without him to whom one is responsible, for there is no reply where there is not an appeal. In the last resort ' the religious life ' means concreteness itself, the whole concreteness of life *without reduction*, understood dialogically, included in the dialogue.

Man has then always a real function in the dialogue. Something has been allotted to man in however mysterious a way, and that is the initiative.

Man cannot complete, and yet he must begin, in the most serious, actual way. This was once stated by a Chassid in a somewhat paradoxical interpretation of Genesis : ' " In the beginning " —that means : for the sake of the beginning, for the sake of the beginning did God create heaven and earth. For the sake of man beginning, that there might be one who would and should begin in the direction towards God.'

Towards the end of the treatise of the Mishnah[6] which deals with the Day of Atonement there occurs a great saying, which must be understood in the same way as the Chassid understood the words of Genesis. Here Rabbi Akiba speaks to Israel : ' Blessed are ye, O Israel. Before whom do ye cleanse yourselves, and who makes you clean ? Your Father in heaven '. Here is the deed of man both in its reality and in its insufficiency clearly expressed, in the reality of man's action and in his dependence upon grace. And the saying ends pregnant with the meaning which it draws from the daring exegesis : ' HE is the cleansing waters of Israel '.[7]

# 4. Turning

This beginning by man manifests itself most strongly in the process of turning. It is usual to call this ' repentance ', but to do so is a misleading attempt to make it into psychology ; it is better to take the word in its original, literal meaning, for what it refers to is not something which happens in the secret recesses of the soul, to show itself outwardly only in its ' consequences ' and ' effects' ; it is something which happens in the immediacy of the reality in which men and God are together. Turning is as little an event falling within the soul of man as is a man's birth or death ; it comes upon the whole person, it is carried out by the whole person, and does not take place in the intercourse of a man with himself, but in the simple reality of the *ur*-reciprocity.

Turning is a human fact, but it is also a world-embracing power. We are told that when God contemplated creating the world, and sat tracing it on a stone, in much the same way as a master-builder draws his groundplan, then God saw that the world would have no stability. He then created turning, and the world had stability, for when now it was lost in the abyss of its own self, and far off from God, deliverance was open to it, a deliverance which it was mercifully permitted to bring about through its own movement leading it to its complete turning back.

When we consider that turning means something so mighty, we can understand how Adam could learn the power of turning from Cain, we can understand the saying which is reminiscent of a New Testament text, but which is quite independent of it, ' In the place where those stand who have turned, the completely righteous cannot stand.'

Again we see that there is no separate sphere of ethics in Judaism. This, the highest ' ethical ' moment, is fully taken up into the dialogical life between God and man. Turning is not a return to an earlier ' sinless ' state ; on the contrary, it is a turning of the whole individual—the individual being carried on to the way of God in turning round. This ἡ ὁδὸς τοῦ θεοῦ, however, does not merely indicate a way which God recommends to man ; it indicates that he, God himself, walks in his *shekhinah*,[8] in his 'indwelling', through the history of the world ; he treads the way, he takes upon himself the fate of the world. The man who turns finds himself standing in the furrows which the living God himself has made on his way through the world.

When we remember this, we understand the full, pregnant meaning of the word with which the Baptist, then Jesus, then the disciples begin their preaching, the word which is falsely rendered by the Greek μετανοεῖτε referring to a *spiritual* process, but which in the original Hebrew or Aramaic idiom cannot have been anything else than that cry of the prophets of old : ' Turn '. And when we remember this, we can also understand how the following sentence is linked to that beginning of the sermon : ' for the ἡ βασιλεία τῶν οὐρανῶν is at hand ', which, according to the Hebrew or Aramaic usage of the time cannot mean ' Kingdom of Heaven ' in the sense of ' another world ' : *shamajim*, heaven, was at that time one of the paraphrases for the name of God ; *malchut shamajim*, ἡ βασιλεία τῶν οὐρανῶν does not mean Kingdom of Heaven, but the Kingdom of God, which realises itself in the whole of creation, and wills to complete it in this way.   The Kingdom of God is at the hand of man, it wants to be grasped and made actual by him, not through any theurgical act of ' violence ', but through turning of the whole individual ; and not as if he were capable of accomplishing anything through this, but because the world has been created for the sake of his ' beginning '.

## 5.   Against Gnosis and Magic

The two spiritual powers of gnosis and magic, masquerading under the cloak of religion, threaten above all others the insight into the religious reality, into man's dialogical situation.   They do not attack religion from outside, they penetrate to its centre, and there they establish themselves and pretend to be its essence.   As Judaism has always held them at bay and separated itself off from them, its battle has largely fallen within itself.   This battle has often been misunderstood as a battle fought against myth. But only an abstract-theological monotheism can be empty of myth, even dares to see her enemy in it; living monotheism needs it, as all religious life needs it, as the specific forms of remembering in which its central events can be kept safe and remain embodied from generation to generation.

Israel was for the first time confronted with gnosis and magic by its two great neighbouring cultures: Gnosis, the knowledge of the secret which can be learnt, in the Babylonian teaching about the stars whose power holds all earthly destinies to ransom—this was later to reach its full development in the Iranian teaching of the world-soul emprisoned in the cosmos; magic, the knowledge of the secret which can be coerced, in the Egyptian teaching of how death can be conquered and everlasting health attained by the performance of prescribed formulae and gestures. The tribes of Jacob could only become Israel by disentangling themselves from both: He who imagines that he knows and holds fast the secret cannot any longer approach it as his ' you '; and he who thinks that he can cast a spell over it and utilise it is unfitted for the hazards of true reciprocity. The temptation of gnosis is answered by ' the Law ', the Torah,[9] with the cry which supports all later teaching: ' The secret things belong unto the Lord our God: but those things which are revealed belong unto us and to our children for ever, that we may do all the words of this law.' Revelation does not deal with the secret of God, but with the life of man, and it deals with this as with something which can and should be lived facing the secret of God, and turned towards it; even more, it is so lived, when it is the true life of man. And the magical temptation is withstood by the word of God from out of the burning bush:

Moses expected the people in their distress to ask
him, what was the news about the name of the god
as whose messenger he spoke to them (not, which
was the name of the ' God of their Fathers ' !) ;
for, according to the usage common to primitive
peoples, once they seized the secret of the name,
they could cast a spell over the god, and thus
coerce him to manifest himself to them, and save
them.   But when Moses voiced his scruple as to
what reply he should give to the people, God
answers him by revealing even the name, for he
says explicitly in the first person what the name
hides under the form of the third person.   Not
that often stated ' I am that I am ' of the meta-
physician—God does not make theological statements—but he gives the answer which his creatures
need, and which profits them :  ' I shall be there as
he who I there shall be '.   That is: You need not
cast a spell over me, for I am there, I am with you ;
but you cannot even cast a spell over me, for I am
always with you, as I always choose to be with
you ;  I myself do not assume any of my manifestations beforehand ;  you cannot learn to meet
me, you meet me, when *you* meet me—' It is not in
heaven, that thou shouldest say, Who shall go up
for us to heaven, and bring it unto us, that we may
hear of it and do it . . . But the word is very
nigh unto thee, in thy mouth and in thy heart,
that thou mayest do it.'

It is also in the light of its own inner battle
against the infiltration of gnosis and magic that the
dynamic of later Judaism must be understood, and
especially that annoying Talmud.[10]   We can only
grasp what its many apparently pedantic discus-
sions are about when we keep in mind this constant
double threat to the religious reality, the one from
gnosis in the form it took in the late-Iranian teaching of the two principles and the middle-substance,

the other from magic in the form of the Hellenistic practice of sorcery. Both of these amalgamated inside Judaism and became the Kabbalah,[11] this mysteriously powerful undertaking of the Jews to wrest themselves free from the concreteness of the dialogical situation. The Kabbalah was overcome, because it was taken up into the *ur*-Jewish conception of the dialogical life just as it was. This overcoming of the Kabbalah is the important work of Chassidism ; it left all middle-substances to fade before the relationship between God's transcedence, only to be called ' the limitless ' with the suspension of all limited being, and his immanence, his ' indwelling '. The secret of this relationship is, however, no longer one which can be learnt, but it is laid immediately on the pulsating heart of the human person as the *jichud*, as the unification which man must proclaim and make true in all the moments of his life, and in all the things of the world. And Chassidism drains sorcery of its poison by not attempting to deny the influence of humanity on deity. Far above and beyond all formulae and gestures, above all exercises, penances, preparations, premeditated actions, Chassidism proclaims that the influence comes from the one true bearer, the consecration of the whole of the everyday. Thus it drains off the technique underlying the purpose of sorcery, and leaves no specific means behind, no means which are valid once and for all and applicable everywhere. In this way Chassidism renews the insight into the reciprocity where the whole of life is put unreservedly at stake, the insight into the dialogical relationship of the undivided human being with the undivided God in the fullness of this earthly present, with its unforeseeable, ever changing and ever new situations, the insight into that differentiation between ' the secret ' and ' the revealed ', and the union of both in that not to be learnt, but ever to be experienced ' I shall be there ' ; the insight into the reality of the meeting.

Gnosis misreads the meeting ; magic outrages it ; the meaning of revelation is that its place shall be prepared; Chassidism interprets this: That its place shall be prepared in the whole reality of human life.

## 6.  The Triad of Time

The insight which Judaism has with regard to the dialogical situation, or rather the fact that it is completely imbued with it, gives Judaism its indestructible knowledge of the threefold chord in the triad of time : Creation, Revelation, Redemption.

Within early Christianity the Gospel according to John was the first to try to substitute two chords for the three by weaving together revelation and redemption into one.  The light which shone in darkness and was not received by the darkness, the light that enlightens the whole man, that comes into the world—that light is at the same time revelation and redemption, by his coming into the world God reveals himself, and the soul is redeemed.  The Old Testament shrinks into a prologue to the New Testament.  Marcion went further : He tried to substitute one chord for the two by banishing creation from religious reality ; he tore God the Creator apart from God the Redeemer, and declared that the former was not worthy of being adored in prayer, which means that he declared him to have lost his deity.  The ' alien ' God, who reveals himself in redeeming the world, redeems the soul from the cosmos and its builder, who becomes the merely ' righteous '—not ' good '—God of the Jews, the demiurge, and the lawgiver, and the false god of this aeon in one.

The Old Testament was thrown overboard as a book against God. Marcion's work has not been accepted by the Church, which has, indeed, to a large extent fought against it. How present it has remained in Christian thought, however, is shown by Harnack's marcionising thesis, which is only one of many witnesses to this. In his thesis Harnack stamps the ' preservation ' of the Old Testament as a canonical document in Protestantism as ' the consequence of a religious and ecclesiastical attack of paralysis ', and out of the whole of the Old Testament it is only to the prophets that he will allow any religious value. But with the victory of this thesis more would be gained than the separation of two books, and the profanation of one for Christendom : Man would be cut off from his origin, the world would lose its history of creation, and with that its creaturely character ; or, the creation would itself become the Fall ; what exists would not only be shattered cosmologically, but in the last resort, and for religion, it would also be divided beyond possibility of redress, into a ' world' of matter and moral law, and an overworld of spirit and love. Here the Iranian teaching of the two principles finds its Western superstructure, and the duality of man, estranged from his natural, trustful faith in life, its theological sanction. From being the crown of the work of creation, redemption becomes its scaffold ; the world can no longer as such become the Kingdom of God. ' The Unknown ' who is here called upon is the spirit of *reduction*.

For the Western peoples this departure would only have meant a threat of disintegration ; for Judaism it would have meant certain dissolution. What saved Judaism is not, what the Marcionites might well imagine, that it failed to experience ' the tragedy ', the contradiction in the world's history, sufficiently deeply ; but rather that it experienced it in the dialogical situation, which means that it experienced *the contradiction as theophany*. Even this world, even this contradiction, unabridged, unmitigated, unsoftened, unsimplified, unreduced, even this it is which shall be—not overcome—but consummated, yes, consummated in the Kingdom, for it is that, even that with all its contrariety, on which the Kingdom is so founded that all reduction would only hinder its consummation, while all unification of contraries would prepare it, unification through redemption not from evil, but of evil, that evil which is the power which God created for his service, and to do his work.

If it is true that the whole world, all the happenings in the world, the whole world-life without anything subtracted from it, stands in the dialogical situation ; if it is true that the history of the world is a real dialogue between God and his creature, then it is not a trivial, man-made device for his own orientation when he sees this history as differentiating itself and appearing as the triad, but it is actual reality itself. What comes to us out of the abyss of genesis, and into the sphere of our uncomprehending grasp and our faltering narrative is God's cry of creation into the naught. Still yet does silence lie brooding before him, but soon from the midst of the silence things arise and give answer through their very coming into existence ; and when God blesses them, and gives them their appointed work, revelation has begun ; for revelation is nothing else than the relation between giving and receiving, which means that it is also the relation between desiring to give and failing to receive. Revelation tarries until the creature by his turning and by God's redeeming grace answers truly and loudly ; and then the unity emerges, formed out of the elements of contrariety itself, to establish amidst all the undiminished multiplicity and manifoldness the communion of creatures in the name of God and before his face.

As God's cry of creation does not call to the soul, but to all things, as revelation does not take possession of and govern the soul, but all of the human being, so it is not the soul, but the whole of the world, which is to be redeemed in the redemption. Created stands man, a unique physical body, ensouled by his relation to the created, enspirited by his relation to the Creator. To the whole man, in just this his harmony of body, soul, and spirit, comes the Lord of Revelation and lays his message upon the whole man, so that not only with his thought and his feeling, but also with the sole of his foot and the tip of his finger, he may receive the sign-language of the emerging reality. In the unique corporeal life must the redemption take place. Not less than the whole of his creation will God the Creator consummate ; not less than the whole of his revelation will God the Revealer make actual ; not less than the all in need of redemption will God the Redeemer draw into his arms.

# THE TWO CENTRES OF THE
# JEWISH SOUL

YOU have asked me to speak to you about the soul of Judaism. I have followed this request, although I am against the cause for which you hold your conference, and I am against it not merely ' just as a Jew ', but also truly as a Jew, that is, as one who waits for the Kingdom of God, the Kingdom of Union, and who regards all such ' missions ' as yours as springing from a misunderstanding of its nature, and as a hindrance to its coming. When, in spite of this, I have followed your invitation, then it is because I thought that when one is invited to give out of one's knowledge, one should not ask ' Why have you invited me ? ' but one should give what one knows as well as one can—and that is my intention.

There is, however, one important subject within the sphere of Judaism about which I do not feel myself called upon to speak, and that is ' the Law '. My point of view with regard to this subject diverges widely from that which has been handed down to us ; it is not without its basis of law, but neither is it entirely based on law. For this reason I should neither attempt to present tradition, nor substitute my own personal standpoint for the information you have desired of me. Besides, the problem of the Law does not seem to me to belong at all to the subject with which I have to deal. It would be a different matter were it my duty to present to you the teaching of Judaism. For the teaching of Judaism comes from Sinai ; it is a teaching of Moses. But the *soul* of Judaism was before Sinai ; it is the soul which drew near on Sinai, and there received what it did receive ; it is older than Moses ; it is of the patriarchs, a

soul of Abraham, or, more truly, as it concerns th
*product* of a primordial age, it is a soul of Jacob.
The Law joined itself to it, and it cannot hence-
forth ever again be understood outside of it, but it
itself is not of the Law.   If one wants to speak of
it, one must consider all its transformations down
the ages until this day, but never forget that on
all its stages, it is still always it itself which is on
its way.

This qualification, however, only makes the
task still more difficult.  ' I should try to show you
Judaism from inside ', wrote Franz Rosenzweig
in 1916 to a Christian friend of Jewish descent,
' in the same hymnic way as you might show
Christianity to me, the outsider; but I cannot do
it for the very reasons which make it possible for
you.  The soul of Christianity may be found in
its utterances ;  Judaism wears on its ouside a
hard, protecting shell, and one can only speak about
its soul from inside '.  When, therefore, I still
venture to speak about it here, to the outside world,
it is only because I do not intend to give an account
of its soul, but only some indication of its fundamental attitude.

It is not necessary for me to labour the point
that this fundamental attitude is nothing else than
the attitude of faith, viewed from its human side.
' Faith ', however, should not be taken in the sense
given to it in the *Epistle to the Hebrews*, faith that
God is.   That has never been doubted by the soul
of Jacob : When it proclaimed its faith, its *emunah*,
then it only proclaimed that it put its trust in the
everlasting God, that he would be there with it, as
the patriarchs had experienced he was there with
it ;  and that it entrusted itself to him, to him who
was there with it.   Franz Baader did justice to the
depth of Israel's faith relationship when he defined
' faith as pledge, that is, as a tying of oneself, a
betrothing of oneself, an entering into a covenant.'

The fealty of the Jew is the substance of his soul. The living God to whom he has pledged himself has untold numbers of bearers of his appearance in the infinite variety of things and events ; and this in itself acts both as an incentive and as a steadying influence to those who owe him allegiance. In the abundance of the manifestations they can ever and again know the One to whom they have entrusted and pledged themselves. The crucial word which God himself spoke of this re-finding of his presence was said to Moses from the midst of the burning bush : ' I shall be there as he who I there shall be '. He is ever there, ever present to his creature, but always as he who he is just here and now; the spirit of man cannot foretell in what garment of what being and what situation God will be manifested. It is for man to recognise him in each of his garments. I cannot straightaway call any man a pagan ; I know only of the pagan in man. In so far as there is any paganism, it does not consist in not discerning God, but in not recognising him as the same ; the Jewish in man, on the contrary, seems to me to be the ever renewed re-discernment of God. I shall therefore speak to you about the Jewish soul in reference to its fundamental attitude ; I shall regard it as being the concretion of this human element in a popular form, and consider it as the folk-created instrument of such a fealty and re-discernment.

I see the soul of Judaism as turning round two centres like an ellipse.

One centre is the fundamental experience that God is wholly raised above man, that his throne is out of the sight of man, and that yet he is present with these human beings who are absolutely incommensurable with him in an immediate relationship, and that he is turned towards them. To know both at the same time in such a way that they cannot be divided from each other constitutes the life in the very heart of every believing Jewish soul. Both, ' God in heaven ', that is in complete hiddenness, and man ' on earth ', that is in the fragmentariness of his world of sense and understanding ; God in the perfection and incomprehensibility of his being, and man in the fathomless contradiction of this strange existence from birth to death—and between both immediacy.

The pious Jews of pre-Christian time called upon their God as their ' Father ' ; and when the naively pious Jew in Eastern Europe to-day uses this name, he does not repeat something which he has learnt, but he bears witness to a realisation which has grown up in himself of the fatherhood of God and the sonship of man. It is not as if these men did not know that God is also utterly distant ; only, they know at the same time that however far away God is, it never makes him unrelated to them, and that even the man who is farthest away from God cannot cut himself off from the mutual relationship. In spite of the complete distance between God and man they know that when God created man, he set the mark of his image upon his brow, and embedded it in his nature, and that however faint it may become, it can never be wiped out.

When Baalshem according to the Chassidic legend was exorcising the demon Sammael, he showed him this mark on the forehead of his disciples, and when the Master bade the conquered demon begone, the latter prayed, ' Sons of the living God, permit me yet to remain a little while here and look at the mark of the image of God on your faces '. The real commandment of God to men is that they carry this image into life.

' Fear of God ', accordingly, does never mean to the Jews that they shall fear God, but that they shall be aware of his incomprehensibility with trembling. The fear of God is the creaturely knowledge of the darkness to which none of our spiritual powers can reach, but from out of which God reveals himself. Therefore, ' fear of God ' is rightly called ' the *beginning* of wisdom '. It is the dark gate through which man must pass if he is to enter into the love of God. He who wants to avoid passing through this gate, he who thus begins to provide himself with a comprehensible God, who is made thus and not otherwise, runs the risk of having to despair of him in the matter-of-factness of the course of history and of life, or of falling into inner falsehood. Only through the fear of God does man so enter into the love of God that he cannot again be cast out of it. But fear of God is just a gate ; it is not a house in which one can comfortably settle down—he who should want to live in it would in adoration neglect the performance of the real commandment. God is incomprehensible, but he can be known in the bond of mutual relationship with him. God cannot be fathomed by knowledge, but he can be imitated. The life of man who is so unlike God can yet be lived in *imitatione Dei*. To him, the unlike, is yet ' the likeness ' not closed. It is utterly serious when Scripture adjures man to walk in God's path and in his footsteps. Man cannot in his own strength complete any path or any stage of the path, but he can enter on to the path, he can take this first step, and again and again this first step. Man cannot ' be like God ', but in all the inadequacy of each of his hours, he can follow God in each with the capacity he has in that hour—and when he has worked according to the capacity of this his hour, he has done enough. This is not a mere act of faith ; it is a covenant to be living in this hour with all the activity of a created person. Man is able to enter into this convenant : Undistrained and undistrainable is the capacity always

there from generation to generation. No primordial ' Fall ', however far-reaching in its effects,
empowers God to empound this central property
of deciding, for the intention of God the Creator is
mightier than the sin of man. Their knowledge
of creation and of creatureliness tells the Jews that
there may well be burdens that are inherited from
pre-historic and historic times, but that there is
no overpowering original sin which could prevent
him, the late-comer, from deciding as freely as did
Adam ; as freely as Adam let God's hand go, so
freely can he, the later-comer, clasp it. We are
referred to grace ; but we do not do God's will,
when we take it upon ourselves to begin with grace
instead of beginning with ourselves. Our beginning, our having begun, even this in its poverty,
and only this, leads us to grace. God has not
made tools for himself, he needs none ; he has
formed for himself a partner in the dialogue of
time, a partner who is capable of holding converse.

In this conversation God speaks to man with
the life which he gives him, and which he gives him
again and again. Therefore, man can only answer
God with the whole of life—with the way in which
he lives this life that is given him. The Jewish
teaching of the wholeness of life is the other side
of the Jewish teaching of the unity of God. Because God bestows on man not only spirit, but the
whole of his existence, from its ' lowest ' to its
' highest ' levels, man cannot fulfil the obligations
of his partnership with God by any spiritual
attitude, by any worship, in any superstructure of
holiness ; the whole of life is required, with all its
facts, and in all its circumstances. There is no
true, human share of holiness outside the hallowing
of the everyday. In so far as Judaism unfolds itself
in the history of its faith, and so long as it does unfold itself in that, it holds ever out against ' religion '
as being the attempt to assign a circumscribed

part to God in order to satisfy him who speaks and lays claim to the whole. And this unfolding of Judaism is really an unfolding, and not a metamorphosis.

To make clear what is meant by this we may take the sacrificial cultus as our example. One of the two fundamental elements in the biblical animal sacrifice is the sacramentalising of the natural life: He who slaughters an animal consecrates a part of it to God, and by this he consecrates his eating. The second, fundamental element is the sacramentalising of the complete surrender of life ; to this belong all the types of sacrifice in which the person who offers the sacrifice puts his hands on the head of the animal in order to identify himself with it ; in doing so he gives physical expression to the fact that he intends to bring himself, when he brings the animal. He who performs these sacrifices without this intention, without preparing his soul, makes the cultus meaningless, yes, turns it into an absurdity ; it was against him that the prophets directed their fight against the empty sacrificial service. In the Judaism of the Diaspora prayer takes the place of sacrifice ; but prayer is also offered for the reinstatement of the cultus, that is, for the return of the holy unity of body and spirit. And in that achievement of Diaspora Judaism which we call chassidic piety both the fundamental elements unite into a new conception which penetrates to the original meaning of the cultus : When the purified and sanctified man in purity and holiness takes food up into himself, then the eating becomes a sacrifice, the table an altar, and man dedicates himself to the Deity. Here there is no longer any gulf between the natural and the sacramental ; and here there is not any longer the need for a substitute ; here the natural event has itself become a sacrament.

What is holy strives to include the whole of life. The Law differentiates between the holy and the profane, but it wants to proceed to the messianic removal of the differentiation, and to the sanctification of everything. Chassidic piety does not any longer recognise anything as straight-out and irreparably profane : ' The profane ' is for it only a name for the not yet sanctified, for that which exists to be made holy. Everything bodily, all drives and urges and desires, everything creaturely, is material for sanctification. From out of the very same powers of passion that give rise to evil when they remain undirected, arise the good when they are turned towards God. Man does not serve God with the spirit only, but with the whole of his nature, without anything subtracted from it. There is not one realm of the spirit and another of nature ; there is only the coming realm of God. What we call spirit, and what we call nature, hail both equally from the God who is above both and equally unconditioned by both, and whose kingdom reaches its fulfilment in the complete unity of spirit and nature.

The second centre of the Jewish soul is the deep consciousness that God's redeeming power is working everywhere and at all times, and that yet nowhere and at no time is there a state of redemption. The Jew experiences as a person what every open-hearted human being experiences as a person: In the hour when he is most utterly forsaken there comes the breath from above, the nearness, the touch, the mystery of light out of darkness ; and the Jew, as part of the world, experiences, perhaps more intensely than any other part, the world's lack of redemption. He feels its unredeemed state against his skin, he tastes it on his tongue, the burden of the unredeemed world rests on him. On the background of this his well-nigh physical knowledge he *cannot* concede that the redemption has taken place ; he knows that it has not. It is true that he can discover the pattern of redemption in the history that has passed, but always only that mystery of light out of darkness which is at work everywhere and at all times ; not any redemption of any other kind, none which by its nature would be unique, which would be conclusive for future ages, and which only just had to be consummated. Besides, it would only be through a denial of his own mind and his own calling that it would be possible for him to acknowledge that in a world which still remains unredeemed, an anticipation of the redemption had been brought about by which the human soul—or really only the souls of men who are believers in a definite sense—had been redeemed. With a strength which original grace has implanted in him, and which nothing that has happened throughout the ages has succeeded in wresting from him, the Jew defends himself against the radical division between soul and world which forms the basis of this conception ; he defends himself against the picture of a divine fissure in the existing world ; he defends himself passionately against the fearful notion of a *massa perditionis*. The God in whom he believes has not created the all in order to let it split asunder into a blessed and a damned half, God's eternity is not to be conceived by man ; but—and this we Jews know until the moment of our death—there cannot be any eternity in which not *everything* would be taken up into God's atonement, when he has drawn time back into eternity. Should there, however, be a stage in the redemption of the world, in which redemption fulfils itself first in one part of the world, then we do not derive any claim from our faith to our being redeemed, much less do we derive any claim from any other source. ' And if you will not yet redeem Israel, then redeem at any rate the Gojim '' the Rabbi from Kosnitz used to pray.

It is possible to advance the argument against me that, after all, there has been another eschatology in Judaism than the one to which I have pointed, that beside the prophetic eschatology stands the apocalyptic eschatology. It is in actual fact important to make clear to oneself where the difference between them lies. The prophetic belief about the end of time is in all essentials autochtonous, the apocalyptic belief is in all essentials built up of elements from Iranian dualism. Accordingly, the former promises a consummation of creation, the latter its abrogation and supersession by another world completely different in its nature ; the former lets the still swirling powers, ' the evil ', find the direction towards God, and enter into the good ; the latter sees at the end of days good and evil severed for ever, the one redeemed, the other for all eternity unredeemed ; the former believes that the earth shall be saved, the latter despairs of that which it considers to be lying in perdition ; the former lets God's creative, original will fulfil itself without remainder ; the latter lets the unfaithful creation have power over the creator in that it forces him to sacrifice nature. There was a time, when it must have seemed uncertain, whether the current apocalyptic teaching would not be victorious over the traditionary, prophetic messianism ; if this had happened, it seems certain that Judaism would not have outlived its central faith—explicitly or imperceptibly it would have become one with Christianity, which is so strongly influenced by that dualism. During an epoch without prophets the Tannaites[2] helped the prophetic messianism to triumph over the apocalyptic conception, and in doing so they saved Judaism.

Still another important difference divides the two forms of Jewish belief about the end of time. The apocalypts want to predict an unalterable, immovable, future event ; on this point also they move within Iranian conceptions, for, according to the Iranians, history is divided into equal cycles of thousands of years each, and the end of the world, the final victory of good over evil, can be predetermined with mathematical accuracy. Not so the prophets of Israel: They prophesy 'about those who turn ', that is, they do not warn against something which will happen in any case, but against what will happen, if those who are called upon to turn do not do so. *The Book of Jonah* gives a clear example of what is meant by prophecy. After Jonah has in vain tried to flee from the task God has given him, he is sent to Nineveh to prophesy its destruction. But Nineveh turns—and God changes its destiny. Jonah is vexed that the word, for whose sake the Lord broke down his resistance, has now been rendered void : If one is forced to prophesy, then one's prophecy must stand ; but God is of a different opinion ; he will not employ soothsayers, but messengers to the souls of men—to the souls of those men who are able to decide which way they should go, and whose decision is allowed to contribute to the forging of the world's fate. Those who turn co-operate in the redemption of the world.

Man's partnership in the dialogue finds here its highest form of reality. It is not as if any definite act done by man could draw grace down from heaven ; and yet, grace answers deed, in unpredictable ways, it is not to be reached, and yet it does not withhold itself. It is not as if man has to do this or that to hasten the redemption of the world—' he that believeth shall not make haste ', and yet those who turn co-operate in the redemption of the world. The participation which has been assigned to the creature is a mystery. ' Does that mean that God cannot redeem his world without its help ? It means that God would not even do that. Has God need of man for his work ? He wills to have need of man.'

He who speaks of activism in this connection misunderstands the mystery. The act is no outward gesture. ' The shofar ', says a haggadic[3] word, ' which God will blow on that day will have been made out of the right horn of the ram which once took Isaac's place as sacrifice '. The 'servant' whom God made ' a polished shaft ' to hide him, obviously unused, in his quiver, the man who is condemned to live in hiddenness—or rather, not one man, but the type of men to whom this happens, and who arise in generation after generation—the man who is hidden in the shadow of God's hand, who ' does not cause his voice to be heard in the street ', he who suffers for God's sake, unesteemed by men, he, even he it is, who has been given as light for the tribes of the world, that God's ' freedom may be unto the end of the earth '

The *mysterium* of the act, of the human part in preparing the redemption, walks through the shadow of the ages as a *mysterium* of seclusion, also in relation to the person himself, until one day it will come forth into the open. To the question why tradition made the Messiah be born on the anniversary of the day of the Destruction of Jerusalem, a chassidic rabbi answered : ' The power cannot arise, unless it has dwelt in the great seclusion . . . In the vessel of oblivion grows the power of remembrance. That is the power of redemption. On the day of the Destruction the power lies in the ground and grows. Therefore, on this day do we sit on the ground ; therefore, on this day do we visit the graves ; therefore, on this day will the Messiah be born '.

These two centres of the Jewish soul continue to exist, also for the ' secularised ' Jew, in so far as he has not lost his soul, although for him they have been robbed of their real names. They are, the immediate relationship to that which is, and the atoning power at work in an unatoned world ; in other words, the non-incarnation of God who reveals himself to ' the flesh ', and is present with it in a mutual relationship ; and the unbroken continuity of human history, where human beings turn towards the fulfilment, and always in doing so experience this power of deciding. These two centres it is which form the ultimate division between Judaism and Christianity.

We ' unify ' God, when, living and dying, we acknowledge his unity; we do not unite ourselves with him. The God in whom we believe, to whom we are pledged, does not join himself to human substance on earth. But just this that we do not imagine that we can unite ourselves with him enables us so ardently to demand ' that the world shall wholly be set in the royal domain of the Mighty '.

We feel the salvation happen ; and we feel the unsaved world. For us, at no definite point in history, has a savoiur appeared, so that a new, redeemed history began with him. Because we have not been stilled by anything which has happened, we are wholly orientated towards the coming of that which shall come.

Thus divided from you we have been assigned to you for your help. As Franz Rosenzweig wrote in the letter which I have already quoted : ' You who live in an *ecclesia triumphans* need a silent servant who reminds you every time you believe you have partaken of God in bread and wine, " Sir, remember the last things ".'

What have you and we in common ? When we take the question literally, a book and an expectation. To you the book is a forecourt; to us it is the Holy of Holies. But in this place we can dwell together, and together we can listen to the voice that speaks there. This means that we can work together to bring out the hidden speech of that voice ; together we can loosen the chains of the imprisoned, living word.

Your expectation refers to a second coming, ours to a coming which has not been forestalled. To you the phrasing of the music of world-history sounds as coming from one, absolute middle-point, the year nought ; to us it is an unbroken flow of tones, following each other without a pause, streaming from an original source to a consummation. But together we can wait for the advent of the One, and there are moments when together we may prepare the way before him.

Until the Messiah comes, our destinies divide us. Until then the Jew is to the Christian the incomprehensibly obdurate man, who will not see what has happened ; and the Christian is to the Jew the reckless man, who in an unredeemed world affirms that its redemption is accomplished. This is a gulf which no human power can bridge. But it does not prevent the common watch for a unity coming from God to us, which, soaring above all your comprehension and all our comprehension, affirms and denies, denies and affirms, what you hold and what we hold, and which substitutes for the credal truths of earth, the ontological truth of heaven : Which is one.

You and we, each of us, it behoves to hold inviolably fast our own true faith, that is : our own deepest relationship to truth ; and you and we, each of us, it behoves to show the religious respect for the true faith of the other. This is not what is called ' tolerance ', it is not in doing this that we tolerate the waywardness of the other ; it is to acknowledge the real relationship in which the other stands to truth. Whenever we, Christian and Jew, care more for God himself than for our pictures of God, we are united in the feeling that our Father's house is differently constructed than our human models leave us to think.

# IMITATIO DEI

*They imitate God's mercy.*
Aristides of Athens about the Jews

## 1

IN Plato's *Theaitetos*[1] Socrates declares that evil can never vanish from our world. It is needed as the opposite of good, and as it has no place with the gods, it must dwell with men, and, this being so, we had better make haste to flee from here to there. The way of this flight is, however, to become as like God as it is possible for us ; and that means to become just and pious through knowledge.

It is probably correct to trace this doctrine to the Pythagorean school, to which is ascribed the phrase ' follow after God ',[2] and about whose founder it is said[3] that the whole of his life and that of his disciples was directed towards this ' following after God '. Plato too uses the conception of following after ; he even repeats it, as for instance when he says in the *Phaidros*[4] that only the soul which best follows after God and is most like him shall see true being.

We can only fully understand what is meant here by ' following after God ' and ' becoming like him ', when we recall the Pythagorean conception of metempsychosis as developed by Plato. The soul is a fallen, godlike being, which has been enclosed in the tomb of its body as a punishment for its guilt, and which must migrate through the bodies of animals and men ; if the souls make themselves pure on their way through different bodies, and win back their godlikeness, then they set themselves free from the compulsion to re-enter the corporeal life, and enter anew the world of the gods. God is then the model of the souls who purify themselves in order to return home.

God—but what kind of god is this? When these philosophers from Pythagoras to Plato say ' God ', ' the God ', what do they mean by it, and whom do they mean by it? In order to imitate God one must know him—who is he? ' Zeus, the great leader in heaven ', says Plato in the speech I have already quoted. But who is Zeus?

When we put this question to ourselves, the first thing that comes to mind is the statue by Pheidias of the Throning Zeus, made out of gold and ivory, with the wreath of olive-leaves on his head, the goddess of victory standing in his right hand, and in his left the sceptre wrought out of all metals, with the eagle, the animal forms, the bloom of flowers on his robe ; it is the statue which, as Pausanias[5] tells us, the God himself ratified with a roar of thunder in answer to Pheidias' prayer. But from whence did Pheidias take the conception? Tradition[6] makes him answer the question of his model by saying that he has kept to the model given in the famous verses of Homer's *Iliad*[7] in which the ruler is depicted with his dark brows nodding assent, and the ambrosial locks flowing waving down from his immortal head. When one thinks of all the tales in this same *Iliad* in which Zeus behaves as often like a raving pre-historic giant as like the majestic Olympian,[8] one feels the full influence which the artistic *selection* had in classical statuary. And one further understands from this how Zeus is the wishful creation of the Greek longing for the ideal, perfected by the elimination of all inadequacy. The imagination which on all sides besets the creation of this form tears away from him his original demonic character, such as survived in the snake-bodied Zeus Ktesios, and, by separating off all which does not conform

to the desired picture, makes the pure image stand
out clearly. Although even before this happened,
the longing for the ideal, finding no fulfilment in
form and line, had given expression to the fine
words in the *Heliads* of Aeschylos[9] which dissipate
all form and shape, ' Zeus is all, and that which
rules over all '. From here the way leads irresist-
ibly on to that complete dissolution of the person,
even of the substance itself, which we find in the
prayer which Euripides puts into the mouth of the
Queen of the Trojans, ' Whoever you are, O Zeus,
you who are hard to espy—necessity of things to
be or spirit of man, to you I flee ! '[10] But the
plastic art, the truest task-mistress of the Greek
idea, defies its destiny and, unconcerned about the
undermining act of the tragic writer, she makes the
form conclusively visible, and with that imitable.
Only then can the Platonic mimesis arise out of the
Pythagorean ' following after '. However ' in-
corporeal ' Platonism, especially later Platonism,
thought to make its god, it cannot pry him loose
from the sensuous world of Pheidias, who completed what form and shape had in them to become.
The fact that the god is an ideal that may be followed after remains founded on the fact that he is
an image, a figure created by desire. The Greeks
can only imitate what they themselves have created.

## 2

' Be ye therefore followers of God, as dear
children ; and walk in love, as Christ also hath
loved you ', it says in the letter which the Apostle
Paul wrote to the Ephesians[11]. The imitation of
God is for Christianity identical with the imitation
of its Founder, who presents to it the Deity in a
human form and in a human life, as theG ospel of
John lets the Founder himself say in the words,
' he that hath seen me hath seen the Father '.[12]

These words, taken together with the repeated call
' Follow me ', give the inner meaning of the
tendency within Christianity called the *imiatio
Christi*. It arose in the early days of Christianity
to reach its height more than a thousand years
later ; it did not, however, find its mature, literary
expression until the fifteenth century, and since
then its influence has continued only in isolated
and solitary lives.

Polycarp, Bishop of Smyrna in the first half of
the second century, was a man without any outstanding spiritual gifts, but his strength of character
and trustworthiness made him appear so important
that the great Ignatius wrote to him that the age
desired after him that it might reach unto God.
In his *Epistle to the Phillipians*, Polycarp urges them
to be imitators of the sufferings of Jesus, or rather,
of his readiness to suffer.[13] It was not only from
written tradition that Polycarp had received
information of the characteristic, and the deeds
flowing from it, which he now desired the Phillipians to imitate ; he had received the information
in his youth by mixing with people who had been
eye-witnesses of how his Master lived and died.[14]
This information did not merely transform itself
in him into his demand on the Phillipians, it
determined his own living and dying. Of his
conduct before his martyrdom[15] we are told that
when the populace in the amphitheatre clamoured
for him to be thrown to the lions, he neither fled
nor gave himself up, but proceeded to a country-
farm and tarried there ' to be betrayed ', as he had
been told that Jesus did. It is thus not surprising
that in a writing describing his death one· of his
fellow-Christians counted him among ' the
witnesses and imitators '.[16]

The tendency to imitation realised itself in
Francis of Assissi. ' The imitation of Christ's
life of poverty ' is the watchword of his Order.

In the introductory section to the first Rule he wrote down for his Order, he states that its aim is to follow in the footsteps of Jesus. From the time of his conversion he gave up his own person to this aim, joining himself to Christ's acts and sufferings in the most completely direct way. But the account of his life given by legend shows better than anything else what had grown out of the tendency to imitation during these more than thousand years. Legend describes the similarity between the appearance of Francis of Assissi and that of Jesus ; it draws the similarity out into great and small details, it often carries it through to ' parallels ' that border on the trivial, finally to culminate in the account of the stigmatisation, which becomes the physical embodiment of the tendency round which miracle-stories gather. In ways such as these legend made Francis the *signaculum similitudinis vitae Christi.*[17] Instead of the ethico-religious urge to imitation comes a transformation, a mystical being conformed to Jesus, which indeed in individual cases almost verges on the magical ; instead of the *Christo conformiter vivere* of Bonaventura comes a hundred years later the *Register* of the miraculous *conformitates* of Bartholomaeus de Pisis, whose book *Liber conformitatum* Luther, as is well-known, introduced as the book of ' the Barefooted Monks Eulenspiegel and Alcoran '.

The core of all Christian imitation is after all a memory, a remembrance that is being handed down from one generation to the next ; its character as a core is in no way lessened by the accretion of myth which the process of transmission deposits as the remembrance is handed down. And, moreover, it is a question of the remembrance of a life, of the span of a human life. This double fact— life and remembrance—makes the Christian imitation a complete contrast to the Greek imitation.

In spite of Plato's reluctant remark[18] about the men of Crete, who ' follow after ' Zeus in his more questionable habits, it did not occur to the Greeks ever to incorporate what their myths told them about their highest God into the form which they imitated ; indeed, all the mythical material had to fall away that the form might become a model ; but it was also possible for it to fall away, just because the Greeks were not linked to Zeus by a memory. For the Christian the human life which established him a Christian is the standard and pattern ; he does not imitate a picture, he imitates a life-history.

This insight certainly raises one great question, immediately and strongly : How far can this imitation of a human life be said to be an imitation of God ? The Church answers this question with the dogma of the Incarnation. Other voices come to us from out of the early Christian community. The clearest among these seems to be the one of that Ignatius of Antiochia to whom reference has already been made. He writes in his *Epistle to the Philadelphians* : ' Be ye followers of Jesus Christ, as he was a follower of his Father '.[19] That reminds one strangely of Paul's words to the Corinthians : ' Be ye followers of me, even as I also am of Christ '.[20] The imitation is made easier and more possible by intermediate links. We need only transfer ourselves from mediacy to immediacy, from the imitation of Jesus to his imitation of our Father, and we are standing on Jewish soil.

### 3

The imitation of God, and of the real God, not of the wishful creation ; the imitation not of a mediator in human form, but of God himself— that is the central paradox of Judaism.

A paradox, for how should man be able to

imitate God, the invisible, incomprehensible, un-
formed, not to be formed ? One can only imitate
that of which one has an idea—no matter whether
it be an idea springing from imagination or from
memory ; but as soon as one forms an idea of God
for oneself, it is no longer he whom one con-
templates, and an imitation founded on this idea
would be no imitation of him.

On what can the imitation of God be founded ?

In so far as we can draw conclusions from the
words of Haggadah, the answer given by Jewish
teaching is this :

It is founded on the fact that we are destined
to be like him.

The Midrash[21] interprets the saying of Moses,
' and ye are this day as the stars of heaven for
multitude ' ' by taking the word *rab*, here translated multitude, in its sense of ' Lord, Master ',
and reads, ' To-day are ye like the stars, but in the
world to come ye are destined to be like your
Lord '.[22] And in still stronger language does the
Midrash[23] complete another passage in the same
book (4.4) : ' But ye that did cleave unto the Lord
your God are alive every one of you this day ', it
interprets: ' In this world does Israel cleave unto
the Lord, but in the world to come they will be
his and like him '.

But has then the world to come, ' the world of
fulfilment ', become so divided from the present
world, ' the world of want ', that no bridge of
thought can any longer lead from here across to
there ? It is plainly impossible for us to comprehend that we shall be like God ; and it is really
most comprehensible to us that we are unlike him,
in just the way in which such figurines kneaded
out of ' the dust of the earth ' must be unlike the
creator of all things. What human deed could
even in part fill the abyss between that being like
and this unlikeness ?

Yet, the teaching does not remain content with the bare promise.

Rabbi Acha was a contemporary of the Emperor Julian; he was that astounding man who at weddings used to set the bride on his shoulder in order that he might thus dance the holy dance with her, and at his death it was said that the stars shone by day. It was this Rabbi Acha who commented on the verse of Psalm 100, ' Know the Lord is our God, he has made us, we belong to him '[24] by saying, ' He has made us, and we perfect our souls to him '.[25]

We perfect our souls to God. That ' being like ' God is then not something which is unconnected with our earthly life, it is the goal of our life, provided that our life is really a perfecting of our soul to God. And, this being so, we may well add that the perfection of a soul is called its being like God, which yet does not mean any equality, but means that this soul has made actual that image which was granted it. We perfect our souls to God, that means that each of us who does this makes perfect *his* image, his *jechida*, his ' only one thing ', his uniqueness as God's image.

' For in the image of God did he make man '. It is on this that the imitation of God is founded. We are destined to be like him; that means, we are destined to perfect from out of ourselves, in actual life, the image in which we were created, and which we carry in us that we may—not any longer in this life—experience its consummation.

Judaism, which more than any other religion has grasped the seriousness for actual life of the fact that God created man, has also most unequivocally recognised the importance for the life of man of that ' in his image '. To this the word of Rabbi Akiba bears witness, the word which for so long we have not understood in all its profundity, ' Beloved is man, for he was created in the image of God ; but it was by a special love that it was *made known* to him that he was created in the image of God '.[26] That it has been revealed to us that we are made in his image gives us the incentive to unfold this image, and in doing so to imitate God.

God said, ' Let us make man in our image, after our likeness ' ; but about the creative act itself it is said, ' So God created man in his own image ' ; the image alone is mentioned here, and not also the likeness. How are we to understand that ? A haggadic interpretation[27] answers the question thus : ' In image alone and not also after likeness, because the likeness lies in the hand of man '. The ' likeness ' is to become like.

The Fall of the first human beings consisted in their wanting to reach the likeness intended for them in their creation by other means than by perfecting ' the image '.

' The fundamental reason for the creation of man ', says a chassidic book,[28] ' is that he assimilates himself to his creator as much as he possibly can '. The book further adduces the beautiful saying[29] of Rabbi Chiskijas, the son of Rabbi Chijas : ' Blessed be the pious heralds who liken the image to its creator and the plantation to its planter ', and explains it in the following manner : ' They make themselves like their creator, when they unify all their members to his unity, and drive all parts of evil out of themselves that they may be perfect with HIM their God . . . It was that this might happen that God said, " Let us make man in our image, and after our likeness "—out of love did he create man in his image, so that with the image man should be able to assimilate himself to his creator '.

Again the question which we seemed to have mastered rises up before us : How can we imitate God ? True, his image has been laid in us, has

been outlined in us, and because this is so, we can
rest assured that the goal exists, and that it is
possible to walk the way. But what is the way ?
Have we to fasten our attention on our soul alone,
on its hidden image, which we have been commanded to unfold ? Or have we a model of what
we should unfold and perfect it into ? Is God
our model ? And yet again : ' How can he, the
incomprehensible, be that ?

And again the answer comes from one of the
masters of the Talmud, this time from the Mishnah,
from some one who lived after the death of Hadrian,
and who was a still more remarkable man than
Rabbi Acha, from Abba Shaul. He was a giant in
stature, by profession a baker in the house of the
patriarch ; he gave himself up above all else to the
fulfilment of the *mizwah*,[30] in pursuance of which
he buried the dead, and he could tell of strange
observations he made in this work ; he was withal
a man of prayer, and interpreted, obviously from
personal experience, the word of the Psalm (10.17) :
' YOU have heard the demand of the humble, you
establish their heart, you cause your ear to hear '
by saying that the granting of the prayer became
manifest in the establishing of the heart. It was
he who used to comment[31] on the word of God :
' Ye shall be holy : for I the Lord your God am
holy ' by saying : ' The royal retinue (really family,
*familia*) it behoves to imitate the King '. But
another saying leads us even deeper into his conception of the *imitatio Dei*. He starts from a
verse of the song which Moses and all Israel sang
when they had passed through the sea : ' *zeh eli
weanwehu* ', which is to be rendered : ' This is my
God, and him will I praise '. But Abba Shaul
takes the contested word *weanwehu* in a different
sense[32] : ' I will be like him ', or ' I will assimilate
myself to him '. Rashi[33] explains the reason for
this interpretation :[34] Abba Shaul resolved the

word *weanwehu* into its two component parts
*ani wahu*,[35] and interpreted it according to this as
' I and he ', and said : ' I will become like him ',
or, as Rashi expresses it, ' I will form myself after
him to cleave to his ways '. And, in fact, Abba
Shaul continues : ' As he is merciful and gracious,
so be you merciful and gracious '.

To imitate God, means then, to cleave to his
ways, to walk in his way. These are not the ways
which God has commanded man as man to walk in,
they are really God's own ways. But, yet again,
the old question comes back in a new form: How
can we walk in his ways? They are past finding out,
and we are told that they are not like our ways!

Abba Shaul indicates already the answer in his
last words ; it is amplified in two explanatory
comments on the words of Deuteronomy[36], which
a spiritual scholar once called ' Israel's book
*de imitatio Dei* '.[37] It says : ' " to love HIM
your God, to walk in all his ways." What are
the ways of God ? Those which he himself proclaimed to Moses : " Godhood, merciful, gracious,
long-suffering, abundant in loving-kindness and
faithfulness.' " Still more explicit is yet another
saying. It says : (Deut 13.5) : ' HIM your God
shall ye walk after ' ;[38] how should man be able
to walk in the footsteps of the Glory ? Is it not
written (Deut. 4.24) : ' HE your God is a con-
suming fire '. But it is meant in this way : follow
after the *middoth*,[39] the ' attributes ', still better,
the ways in which God works as these are made
known to man. As he clothed the nakedness of
the first human beings, as he visited the sick
Abraham in the grove at Mamre (according to
tradition Abraham was there at the time when he
was suffering after his circumcision), as he comforted Isaac with his blessing after Abraham's
death, until the last act of God in the Pentateuch:
As he himself buried Moses—all these are enacted

*middoth*, visible patterns for man, and the *mizwoth* are *middoth* made human. ' My handicraft ', as the Midrash[40] lets God say to Abraham, ' is to do good—you have taken up my handicraft '.[41]

The secret of God which stood over Job's tabernacle (Job 29.4), before it increased fearfully into suffering and questioning for him, can only be fathomed by suffering, not by questioning, and man is forbidden to pry into and imitate these secret ways of God. But God's handicraft, his revealed way of working, has been laid upon us, and set up for us, as a pattern.

Thus it was not vouchsafed to Moses to see God's ' face ', but he learnt his ' ways ', which God himself proclaimed, passing by before him ; and this proclamation God calls the proclamation of his ' name '.

But where are the revealed ways of God's working revealed ?

Exactly at the beginning of the wandering through the desert ; exactly at the height of Job's trial ; exactly in the midst of the terror of the other, the incomprehensible, ununderstandable works; exactly from out of the secret. God does not show mercy and grace alone to us, it is terrible when his hand falls on us, and what then happens to us does not somehow find a place *beside* mercy and grace, it does not belong to the same category as these, the ultimate does not belong to the attribute of righteousness—it is beyond all attributes. It is indeed the secret, and it is not for us to enquire into it. But just in this, just from out of this, just carried by this, is God's handicraft manifested upon us, manifested and revealed. Only when the secret no longer stands over our tabernacle, but has shattered it, do we learn to know— what remains hidden from the world, but what is open to us—God's intercourse with us. And we learn to imitate God.

# BIBLICAL LEADERSHIP

I do not imagine that you will expect me to give you some character-sketches of biblical leaders. It would be an impossible undertaking, for the Bible does not concern itself with character, nor with personality, and one cannot draw from it any description of characters or personalities. The Bible depicts something else, namely, persons in situations. The difference between these persons means nothing to it, but the difference between the situations in which the person, the creaturely person, the person who is at stake, survives or fails, is all-important to it.

But neither can it be my task to delve beneath the biblical account to a historically more trustworthy picture, to historical data, out of which I could piece together a historically useful, historically stable, picture. For this also it is impossible to do. It is not that the biblical figures are unhistorical. I believe that we are standing at the beginning of a new era in biblical studies; whereas the past era did its utmost to prove that the Bible did not contain history, the coming era will succeed in demonstrating its historicity. By this I do not mean that the Bible depicts men and women and events as they are in actual history; rather do I mean that its descriptions and narratives are the organic, necessary, legitimate ways of giving an account of what existed and what happened. I have nothing against these narratives being called myths and sagas, so long as it is remembered that myths and sagas are essentially memories, actual memories, which are actually conveyed from person to person. But what kind of memory is it which manifests itself in these accounts? I say again

44

memory not imagination, but memory. It is organic memory, an organic memory which moulds and shapes its material. We know of it to-day, because sometimes, though indeed in unlikely and indeed in incredible ways, the existence of great poets with such organic memories still penetrates into our time. If we want to distinguish between authors, between a great author and a prominent, very talented author, the best way is to consider how the one and how the other handle the events of their own lives. The great author leaves the events to drop into him as they happen, unconcerned, trusting, with faith. And the memory does its duty, it moulds organically, without voluntary interference, without fantasy, what has thus been dropped into it, to a valid whole of narrative, or of story ; on which then, admittedly, a great deal of conscious work has to be done, but the distinguishing mark was put upon it by the freely shaping memory. The other author registers, he makes an inventory in what also he calls memory, but which is really something quite different ; he preserves the events while they are happening in order to be able to draw them out unaltered,when he needs them. Well, he will certainly draw them out of the preserving-can unaltered after a fashion, and useful after a fashion, and then he can do with that what he can do.

I said that the great poets show us what takes place in the rise of myths and sagas. Each myth, also the myth which we usually call the most fantastic, is creation round a memory core, round the kernel of the organically shaping memory. It is not that people to whom something has happened like the leading out of Egypt subsequently stretch events, leaving their fantasy to invent elements which they do not remember, and ' embroider ' on what happened ; it is rather that what happened continues to function, the event itself is still active and at work in the souls, but these souls, this common soul, is so made that its memory is formative, myth-creating, and the work which the biblical writers have to do is then to work on the product of this memory. Nowhere is there any point where one could establish conscious alteration, or interference by alien elements ; it is done with true tools.

Because it is all done in this way, we cannot disentangle the historical and biblical material. The power of the biblical writing, which springs from this shaping memory, is so great, the fundamental nature of this memory is so mighty, that it is quite impossible to extract any so-called historical matter from the Bible. The historical matter thus obtained would be unreal, amorphous, without significance. But it is also impossible to distil ' the historical matter ' for another reason. Contrary to other sacred writing of history, undertaken by other nations, there does not exist in the case of Israel any evidence from profane parallels by which one might correct the sacred documents ; there is no other histography written from another point of view than that which resides in the shaping memory ; and this shaping memory stands under a law. It is this law which I shall try to elucidate by the examples with which I deal to-day.

In order to bring out still more clearly and exactly what I have in mind, I may perhaps first recall to you one of the nations with whom Israel came into historical contact and dispute ; I do so for the purpose of considering the aspect under which this nation must have regarded one of the biblical leaders. Let us try to imagine how one of the nations against whose kings Abraham fought must have regarded Abraham. The account to which I refer occurs in *Genesis*, chapter 14, a chapter whose fundamental historical character seems to me beyond doubt. Undoubtedly Abraham was

a historical figure to this nation in the same sense
in which we usually speak about history to-day.
But he was no longer Abraham. That which is
important for us about Abraham, that which makes
him a biblical character, a ' Father ', that which is
the reason why the Bible tells us about Abraham,
that is no longer contained in this aspect, the
significance of the figure has evaporated. Or, take
for instance the Egyptians and Moses, and imagine
how an Egyptian historian would have described
Moses and his cause. Nothing of the character
would have been left ; it would be a skeleton
taking the place of the living person.

Therefore our aim can only be to enter into the
Bible, to point to the Bible, to point to that which is
characteristic of the biblical leader in the way in
which the Bible without extraneous influence tells
of him and thinks of him, while we keep ourselves
under the law of its conception of history, its
historical living, which is unlike everything which
we are accustomed to call history. But from this
historical law, from this biblical way of regarding
leader and leadership, different from all other ways
in which leader and leadership have been regarded,
from that have we, from that has Judaism, arisen.

As I wish now to investigate the question of the
essence of biblical leadership, I must exclude from
the enquiry all those figures who are not biblical
leaders in the strictest sense of the term, and that
means, characteristically enough, all those figures
who appear as continuators, all those persons who
are not called, elected, appointed anew, as the
Bible says : by God expressly, but who enter upon
a task already begun without any personal call—
whether it is the person in office who is not permitted to finish the task, and hands over his office
to one of his disciples, breathing upon him the
spirit in the same way as it was breathed upon
him, letting it flow on to his head ; or whether it

is an elected, called, originally anointed king who begets a son that succeeds him without receiving any other anointing than the already customary, official one, which is thus no longer the anointing that comes upon a person, and turns him into another man.

Thus I do not take up for consideration figures like Joshua and Solomon, because the Bible has such figures in common with history—they are figures of universal history. Joshua is a great army-leader, a great conqueror, but a historical figure like any other, with only special religious obligations added to him, obligations which, however, do not colour and characterise the person. Solomon is an oriental king, only just a very wise one ; he does his task, he builds the Temple, but we are not made to see that this task colours and determines him. What has happened here is exactly what we sketched above, the completion of a task, the completion of an already begun, already planned task has been taken over by a disciple or a successor. The task of Moses, which he was not allowed to finish, was taken over by Joshua ; the task of David, which he was not allowed to finish, was taken over by Solomon. In this connection the words recur to me which were exchanged between David and God in the *Second Book of Samuel* about the purpose of building the Temple and the prohibition to carry it out : ' It is not for you ', says God, reproving him as he had reproved Moses, ' it is not for you to bring the people whom you have led, into the land '. The work is taken from them, and, moreover, this is done in view of the special inner and outer situations of these men ; another man has nothing more to do than to bring the work to its conclusion.

Only the elected, only those who begin, are then included in the biblical aspect of leadership. A new beginning may also occur within a series of generations, as for instance within those which we call the generations of the patriarchs ; this is clearly seen in the case of Jacob, with whom something new begins, as the conferring of the new name shows more particularly.

I may first try negatively to characterise the essential features of this biblical aspect of leader. It goes both beyond nature and history. To the men who wrote the Bible, nature, as well as history, each of them, is of God ; and, what is more, each is so deeply a gift of God that the biblical cosmogony gives each separately ; in the first chapter of the creation of the world it is described as the rise of nature ; and then, in the second chapter, this same creation of the world is described as the rise of history. Both come from God, but then the biblical event goes beyond them, God goes beyond them, not in the sense that they, nature and history, become ignored by God and the Bible, but in the sense that both become malleable under God's hand, which takes hold of them, and now so forms, so chooses, so sends, and so orders, as it is not within the laws of nature and history to form, to send, to choose.

I shall here show only by two particularly clear examples what I mean by this. In the first instance, it is the weak and the humble who are chosen. By nature it is the strong, those who can force their cause through, who are able and therefore chosen to perform the historical deeds. But in the Bible those who are chosen are often exactly the younger sons, from Abel, by way of Jacob, of Joseph, of Moses, to David ; and this choosing is accompanied by a rejection, and often a very emphatic rejection, of the older sons; or, those who are chosen are bastards, or of humble origin. And if once in a while a stronger man like Samson appears, a man who has not all these limitations, then his strength is not his own, it is only lent him, not even given him, but really lent him, and he trifles it away, squanders it, in the way in which we are told, only to get it back for the purpose of dying.

A different, but not less telling, expression of what is meant by this peculiar election against nature is given by the battle and victory of Gideon. The Bible makes Gideon do the strangest thing which yet any commander-in-chief has done. He has an army of ten thousand men, and he reduces its numbers again and again till only three hundred men are with him ; and with these three hundred he gives battle, and conquers.

It is always the same story. The purpose of God is done, as the Bible itself says in one place, not by might, nor by power, but ' by my *ruach* ', a word which we can hardly translate ; it is in any case not translated by rendering it ' spirit ' ; the nearest translation of it would be ' with the wind from out of me ', ' with that which moves from out of me '.

It is ' against nature ' that in one way or another the leaders are mostly the weak and the humble. The way in which they carry out their leadership is ' against history '. The moment of success determines for history the selection of events which seem important to it. ' World history ' is the history of successes, and the heroes who have not succeeded, and who cannot be excluded from it on account of their very conspicuous heroism, serve only as a foil, as it were. True, the conquered have also their place in ' world history ' ; but if we scrutinise how it treats the conquerors and the conquered, it becomes abundantly clear which of the two groups it is which is of importance to it. Granted that one takes Croesus together with Cyrus, Herodotus has use for him, that one takes Widukind together with Karl, but only the conquerors are of value to the heart of history. It

croons a low dirge over the overpowered heroes,
but loud does its paean ring for those who stand
firm, who force their cause through, for those who
are crowned with success.   This is ordinary history,
the history which we are accustomed to identify
with what happens, with the real happenings in the
world, and that in spite of the fact that this history
only rests on the particular principle of picking and
choosing, on the selection made by the writer of
history, on the basis of the so-called historical consciousness.

The Bible knows nothing of this intrinsic worth
of success.   On the contrary, when it announces a
successful deed, it is in duty bound to announce
with utmost detail the failure involved in the
success.   When we consider the history of Moses,
we see how much failure is mingled in the one great,
successful action, so much so that when we set the
individual events which make up his history side
by side, then we see that his life consists of one
failure after another, through which runs the thread
of his success.   True, Moses brought the people
out of Egypt, but each stage of this leadership is a
failure.   Whenever he comes to deal with this
people, he is defeated by them, let God ever so
often interfere and punish the people.   And the
real history of this leadership is not the history of
the exodus, but the history of the wandering in the
desert.   But also the personal history of Moses'
own life does not point to his youth and what grew
out of that, it points beyond, to death, to the death
of the unsuccessful man, whose work, it is true,
survives him, but only in new defeats, new disillusionments, and again and again new failures—
and yet also in a hope which is beyond and above
all these failures.

Or, let us consider the life of David.   As we
are told of it, it consists essentially of two great
stories of fleeing.   Before his accession to the

throne there are the manifold accounts of his
flight from Saul, and then follows an interruption,
which is not trifling in length and in value for
profane history, but which in the account appears
paltry enough, and after this there is the flight from
Absolom, painted for us in detail.  But also where
the Bible recounts his triumph, as for instance
with the entry of the Ark into Jerusalem, is this
triumph clearly described as a disgrace in a worldly
sense ; this is very unlike the language of ' world
history '.  What Michal, his wife, says to David
about his triumph, how he ought to have felt
ashamed of himself, behaving like that in front of
his people, that is the language of profane history,
*i.e.*, of history *par excellence*.  To history such a
royal appearance is not permitted, and, rightly so,
seeing that history is what it is.

      And, finally, this glorification of failure cul-
minates in the long line of prophets whose existence
is plain failure.  They live in failure, failure is the
breath in their nostrils, it is for them to fight and
not to conquer ; it is their fundamental experience, it is the fundamental experience of biblical
leadership, of the leadership described by one of
them, a nameless prophet, whose words are preserved in the second part of the *Book of Isaiah*,
where he speaks in the first person of ' the servant
of God ', and lets himself say about God :

> He hath made my mouth like a sharp sword ;
> and yet hath he hid me in the shadow of his hand !
> He hath made me a polished shaft—
> and yet hath he hid me in his quiver !

This existence in the shadow, in the quiver, that is
the final word of the leaders in the biblical world ;
the being enclosed in failure, in obscurity, also
when one stands in the blaze of public life, in the
presence of the whole national life.  In obscurity
is the truth hid, and does yet its work, though,

indeed, in a way far different from that which is known and lauded as effective by world history.

Biblical leadership falls into five basic forms, not so much according to a difference in the personality and character of the leader, I have already said that personality and character do not come into consideration, but according to the difference evinced by the successive situations, the great stages in the history of the people, which the Bible describes, the stages in the dialogue between God and the people. For what the Bible understands by history is a dialogue in which man, in which the people, is spoken to and fails to give answer, and where yet the people from the midst of its failure rises up and tries to answer. It is the history of God's disillusionments, but a history of disillusionments which are a way, so that from disillusionment to disillusionment, over them all, leads the way, the way of the people, the way of man, yes, the way of God through mankind. I said that there are five basic forms in accordance with the successive stages of the situations in the dialogue: First, the patriarch ; secondly, the leader, the leader in the original sense of him who leads on the wandering ; thirdly, the so-called judge ; fourthly, the king, but of course not the king who is a successor, not the king who is a member of a dynasty, but the founder of the dynasty, he who is called, and the first to be anointed ; fifthly, the prophet. All these constitute different forms of leadership in accordance with the different situations.

First the patriarch. This is a current, but not quite correct, conception. No dominion is here exercised, and, when we take the conception in its accurate sense, we cannot here speak of any leadership, for there is as yet no people to lead. The conception indicates a walking ; the way on which the people are to be led begins, exactly from these men. They are Fathers. It is for

them to beget the people. It is this special point in
biblical history, where God, as it were, shortens
his first plan for the whole of mankind, and will
now let a people be born unto him, to the calling
of their appointed work on the completion of the
creation, on the coming of the kingdom. The
fathers of this people are the men of whom I speak.
They are fathers, nothing else. Patriarch says
already too much. They are the real fathers, those
from whom this tribe, this people proceeds, and
when God speaks to them, when God blesses them,
it involves always the same thing, the point is always
conception and birth, always the rise of the people.
And the great story which stands in the middle of
the stories of the patriarchs, the birth and offering
of Isaac, makes exactly this point, in a paradoxical
manner. Kierkegaard has presented this paradox
very beautifully in the first part of his book *Fear
and Trembling*. This paradoxical story of the
second in the line of the patriarchs, of his being
born and very nearly being killed, shows what it
all is about, about begetting, but about the begetting of a people standing at the disposal of God ;
about begetting, but about begetting as a charge.

Now is the people there, and this people is in
bondage. A man receives the charge to lead it
out. That is he whom I have described as the
leader in the original meaning of the word—I have
already said that Joshua is only a continuator—he
is a leader, the leader in the real sense of leader, it
is he who serves in a human way as a tool for the
act which God pronounces, ' I bare you on eagles'
wings and brought you unto myself '. I have
already spoken of his life. But in the middle of
that comes the event, where Moses after the passage
through the Reed Sea[1] intones the song in which
the people joins, and which is the proclamation of
a king. The words with which the song ends
proclaim it, ' King does HE remain in time and in

eternity '. The people has here chosen God himself for its king, and that means that it has created a truth belonging to the lived life out of the tradition of God's kingdom which was common to all semitic peoples, but which never had been taken quite seriously. The leaders are so much in earnest with it that after the land has been conquered, they undertake what is against history, and try to build up a society without a ruling power, without any other ruler than just God. It is the experiment of the primitive theocracy of which the *Book of Judges* tells, and which degenerated into anarchy, as is shown by the examples given in the last part of that Book.

The so-called judge constitutes the third form of leadership. The form is to be understood on the background of an experiment made by the people—we say, the people, but we mean always by it a leading number from among the people who are determined by their desire to make actual the proclamation of God as king, and who try to make the people determined by it. It goes ill with this experiment again and again. Again and again does the people, to use biblical language, fall away from God. But we can also express this in the language of history: The people crumbles again and again ; it is one and the same thing whichever language we use. The attempt to establish a society under no other dominion than that of God, this too can be expressed in the language of history, or, if one likes, in the language of sociology: The experiment to establish a society on pure voluntarism always fails. The people falls away. An invasion made by one of the neighbouring peoples always then succeeds, and Israel, which from a historical point of view is crumbling and disunited, does not stand firm. But in its conquered state it makes itself again subject to the will of God, resolves anew upon God's dominion, and again a divine mission

succeeds, there is always a leader there who is laid
hold of by the spirit, as it laid hold of Moses. This
leader, whose mission it is to free the people, is
' the judge ', or, more correctly, ' he who makes
right ' ; for the people, which after its return to
God now again has right on its side, he makes this
right exist in the actual world, by defeating the
enemy. This is the rhythm in the *Book of Judges* ;
it might almost be called a tragic rhythm, were it
not that the word tragic is so inadequate to the
language of the *Book of Judges*.

But in this Book something new is also being
prepared. The experience of failure, of inability
to bring about this intended, naive, primitive
theocracy becomes ever deeper, ever stronger
grows the demand for a human kingdom. The
Book itself is for its greater part written from an
anti-monarchical standpoint. The kings of the
peoples file before one in a way determined by this
point of view, which reaches its height in that
ironic fable of Jotham's. But in its final chapters
the Book has to acknowledge the failure of the
expectation, because the people is as it is, because
men are as they are. And so kingship is demanded
under Samuel. And it is granted by God. I said
it before, the way leads through the disillusionment.
Thus the demand of the people becomes, as it
were, laid hold of and consecrated from above, for,
by the anointing of the king, a man is transformed
into the bearer of the charge given him ; but this
is not any longer, as was the case with the judge,
a single charge with the completion of which the
leading comes to an end, it is a vice-regal charge
which goes beyond the individual' act, indeed
beyond the life of the individual men. Anointing
may also imply the beginning of a dynasty, when
the king is not deposed by God, as Saul was.

The kingdom is a new stage in the dialogue, a
new stage of attempt and failure, only in this stage

the account lays the blame for the failure on the king, and not any longer, as in the *Book of Judges*, on the whole people. It is no longer those who are led, but the leader himself, who fails, who cannot bear the charge, who does not make the anointing come true in his own person—an *ur*-problem in religious history. All history of great religions, and altogether all great history, hinges on the problem, How do human being endure under that which is here called anointing ?

The history of the kings is the history of the failure of the anointed man to make real his anointing. The rise of messianism, the belief in the anointed king who completes his anointing, is to be understood on the background of this alone.

But now the new, and last, type of leader in biblical history arises in this situation of the kings who fail to answer God, the leader who above all other types is ' against history ', the prophet, he who is appointed to be against the king, against the power, even more, against history, against that which the people calls its historical life. When God says to Jeremiah, ' I give you as a brasen wall against all the land ', then it is really so, the prophet stands not only against the ruler, but against the people itself. The prophet is the man who has been set against his own natural instincts, which bind him to the community, and who likewise sets himself against the will of the people to live on as they have always lived, which, naturally, for the people is identical with the will to live. It goes without saying that not only the rulers, but also the people, treat the prophet as their enemy in the way in which, as a matter of history, it falls to the lot of such men to be treated. These experiences of suffering which thus come upon the prophet unite themselves into that picture of the servant of God, of his suffering and dying for the sake of God's purpose, under whose shadow also Jesus has stood.

When now the Bible tries to look beyond these actual manifestations of leadership to one which no longer obtains in disintegration and failure, when it forms the conception of the messianic leader, it means nothing less by it than that at last the answer succeeds, that from out of mankind itself comes the word, the word which is spoken with the whole being of man, the word which answers God's word. It is an earthly consummation which is waited for, a consummation on this earth, a consummation in and with mankind. But just that is the consummation towards which God presses forward through that which he has created, through nature and through history. This is what the messianic belief means, the belief in the real leader, in the dialogue becoming right, in God's disillusionment being at an end. And when a fragment of an apocryphical gospel makes God say to Jesus : ' In all the prophets I have waited for you, that you would come and I rest in you, for you are my peace ', then this is the late elaboration of a truly Jewish conception.

The biblical question about leadership is concerned with something greater than moral perfection. The biblical leaders are the foreshadowings of the dialogical man, of the man who stands with his whole being in God's dialogue with the world, and who stands firm throughout this dialogue. The life of those people to whom I have referred is consummated by this dialogue, whether it comes in the form of intervention, like Abraham's talk with God about Sodom, or Moses speaking with God after the people's sinning with the golden calf ;  or whether it is the resistance against that which comes upon them and tries to overpower them, and which ends in their submission, as we find it attested from Moses to Jeremiah ;  or whether it is the struggle for purpose and task, as we know it from that discussion

between David and God—in all types it is man's
entry into the dialogue which happens again and
again ; an imperfect entering, but one which is
yet not refused, which yet is set on persevering
in the dialogical world. All that happens is here
experienced as dialogue, what befalls man is taken
as signs, what man tries to do and what ever mis-
carries is taken as attempt and failure to answer,
as the faltering attempts to respond as well as one
can.

Because this is so, biblical leadership always
means a being led. These men are leaders in so
far as they allow themselves to be led, that is, in
so far as they accept that which is offered them, in
so far as they take the responsibility upon them for
that which is entrusted to them, in so far as they
make actual and real that which has been laid upon
them from out of themselves, with their own free
will out of their own being, in the ' autonomy ' of
their person.

So long as we remember this, we can make the
life histories of these leaders intelligible to ourselves.
We see almost always a man being taken out of the
community. God lifts the man out of the community, cuts him off from his natural ties, from
Abraham to Jeremiah must he go forth out of the
land in which he had taken root, away, to the place
where he has to proclaim the name of God ; it is
the same story, whether it is a wandering over the
earth like Abraham's, or a being utterly alone in the
midst of the people like the prophets'. It is an
ever deeper, and indeed ever growing tension from
stage to stage, from situation to situation, in the
relationship between these men and the community. They are either raised up out of their
natural community, or placed against their natural
community, they fight with it, they experience the
contrariety, the contradiction of that which lives,
the contradiction of human existence in this

community, and on the background of it. All this is intensified to the utmost just in the prophets. The great suffering of the prophets, which has been preserved for us by one single one of them, by Jeremiah himself, in a small number of highly autobiographical sayings, just this gives the ultimate form of the tension.

But this ever widening gulf between leader and community, the ever deeper darkness gathering over the leader, the ever greater failure, the ever greater incompatibility of the leader with history in the sense of our current history, this means from the standpoint of biblical history also the growing overcoming of history. What we are accustomed to call history is from the biblical standpoint only the outside of reality. History is the great failure, the refusal of the dialogue, not the failure in the dialogue as given by biblical man, but the refusal of the dialogue, the refusal to enter into the dialogue ; this great refusal is sanctioned in the imposing manner of sanctioning given by so-called history. The biblical point of view repudiates this superficial existence ever more strongly, most strongly in the prophets ; it proclaims that the way, the real way, from the creation to the kingdom is trod not on the surface of success, but in the deep of failure. The real work, from the biblical point of view, is the late-recorded, the unrecorded, the anonymous work. The real work is done in the shadow, in the quiver. The leadership that is public fails more and more, leadership belongs more and more to the secret. The way leads through the work which history does not register, and which history cannot register, which is not entered under the name of him who did the work, but which possibly at some time in a distant generation emerges as done without the name of the doer, the secret working of the secret leadership. And when the biblical writer turns his eyes towards

the final, messianic overcoming of history, he sees
how the outer history becomes engulfed, or rather,
how they both, the outer history and the inner
history, fuse, how the secret which the leadership
had become rises out of darkness and illuminates
the surface of history, as the desire of biblical
history is consummated throughout all the worlds.

# TRUST

THERE are two species of leaders. About one we say, ' I put my faith in him '. About the other, ' I trust him '.

To put one's faith in some one, that is not perchance to think that he always will say or do what is right, but rather that what is not right will be ' right ', namely worthy of approval and imitation, as and when it is *he* who says and does it. Even when one takes pains to prove that he is ' right ', one really knows that one's concern is no longer for what is right and wrong, that is, for a standard outside the person. Truth exists only just by the grace of the person. Therefore it is not truth what one here calls truth.

To trust someone is something else. It means to be convinced that this man whom one trusts stands in a quite definite, positive relationship to truth, to the real truth. In what kind of relationship then ? Surely not as its messenger ? Admittedly not that ; but as its servant. He who serves truth may err as well as other men ; but his errors point towards truth, they are turned towards it, they lead to it. To trust a man, that means to believe in the truth which one can serve, in the truth which does not exist by our grace, but by whose grace we exist.

To put one's faith in man, this is what makes the great fascio of the heathen of all ages and all peoples gather together. To trust man, from this grows up in all ages and among all peoples ' the holy tribe ' of Israel.

I see more and more clearly that we shall find our right way when we substitute trusting human beings for putting our faith in them. We need leaders. But we need leaders whom we do not follow for their sake, but for the sake of the mistress or master whom they serve—whatever they call them. From the kind of service which the leaders give, we see that it is the right one. And if they lack the ability to move the multitude with stirring or commanding words, with a sure touch, inspiring certitude, the unpretentious and most important ability is still theirs, to advise, to exhort, to guide. They set us ever in the presence of the searching beams of truth. They lead in that they teach. Theirs is the secret history of the world.

# INTERPRETATION OF CHASSIDISM

# FOREWORD

Three works from three periods of my life that supplement each other have been collected in this little book. They are, the principal part of the foreword to *The Great Maggid*, written in 1921 ; the introduction to the complete edition of *The Chassidic Books*, written in 1927 ; and a lecture given to the Eranos Conference held in Ascona in 1934. Like my other studies of Chassidism they are not concerned with a historical presentation or an analytical investigation, but with the interpretation of the religious content, and still more of the religious attitude, of Chassidism. Though the three works bear the imprint of their common task, they differ in their approach to the problem. The first considers the chassidic movement principally from the point of view of mankind's way of faith ; the second sets Chassidism in juxtaposition to two earlier manifestations of Jewish, spiritual life, manifestations of an attack on faith, and of a distortion of faith ; the third work is an attempt to compare, on a point of essential importance, the attitude of the faith of the prophets and of the chassids. It is hoped that the joint publication of these three works may help to draw attention to the vital importance of chassidic teaching and chassidic life for present-day Jewry, and for mankind.

# Spirit and Body in the Chassidic Movement

MOVEMENTS which strive for a renewal of the community mean mostly by it that the axe should be put to the root of the present order ; over against the existing order, which they reject, they set quite a different order created by their striving thought. Not so the religious movements which aim at a renewal of the soul. Be the principle which a true, religious movement urges ever so opposed to the state of religion paramount in the environment, the movement feels and expresses this contradiction not as a contradiction of the really existing, original content of tradition; much more does it feel and declare itself as called upon to purify this original content of its present accretions, to restore it, to ' bring it back '. But from this same starting-point the religious movements may proceed very differently in their relation to the prevailing faith. Against and instead of the later stage of tradition the old/new principle may set in a living form its own message ; it will then present its message as the overlaid, original truth which now has been rescued and brought to light, and it will show it to the world in the central man who has been ' sent ' to restore it, and with whom it is indeed identical. In this case the complete separation soon takes place ; such movements may be called movements of foundation. But the principle may also solely go back to an older stage of tradition, to ' the pure word ', which it feels it has to liberate, and against whose distortion it fights. In this case a partial separation takes place ; on the whole the mythico-dogmatic and magic-cultic basis remains untouched, and, regardless of the severance that

67

has taken place in organisation, the spiritual unity continues to exist ; such movements may be called movements of reformation.   But the principle may also accept the tradition with undiminished value in the form which it has ; it will recognise the teaching and dogmas of tradition in their full, contemporary elaboration, without examining their historical credentials, and without comparing them with any original form ; but the principle sheds a new light over the teaching and dogmas, it lets them attain to a new spirituality, to a new meaning, they are renewed by it in their vitality without being changed in their substance.   In this case no separation takes place, though here also the struggle must be kindled between the old and the new, and it may take the most violent forms.   The new community remains within the old community from which it sprang, and tries to penetrate this from within—two forces, the moving force and the constant force, measure themselves against each other, the strife quickly shifts to the ground of the new community itself to continue among its members, indeed even within the heart of the individual himself ; naturally the conditions of the struggle become ever more and more favourable for the force of inertia.   The chassidic movement belongs to movements of this kind.   It proceeded from Podolia and Volhynia about the middle of the eighteenth century ; by the end of the century it had laid hold of Jewry in the whole of the kingdom of Poland, as well as in considerable parts of north-east Hungary and Moldavia ; about the middle of the nineteenth century it had become a spiritually dead, but numerically powerful, movement, which is still in existence to this day.

All true religious movements do not so much desire to offer men the solution of the secret of the world, as they desire to arm them to live by the strength of the secret ; they will not give men instruction in the nature of God, but want rather to show men the way on which they can meet with God. And among these religious movements it is quite specially the third type of which I have spoken that is unconcerned about an omniscient knowledge of nature and command, and deeply concerned about the here and now of the human being, the ever new spring of the eternal truth. It is just for this reason that these movements can take over a system of universal dogmas and precepts from the stage of tradition which is contemporary with them ; their own contribution cannot be codified, it is not the kind of material that lends itself to be embodied in a lasting science or sets of obligations ; it is only light to the seeing eye, strength to the labouring hand, ever appearing anew. This is particularly clearly demonstrated by Chassidism. What existed from of old is not of greatest importance to it, but what happens again and again ; and again, not what happens to man, but what he does, and not the outstanding things he does, but the trivial things ; and much more than what he does, how he does it. Among all movements of this kind none has surely more greatly than Chassidism proclaimed the infinite ethos of the moment.

Chassidism took over two incorporated traditions without essentially adding anything to them beyond a new light and a new strength ; they were, that tradition of religious commandments which is, next to the vedic sacrificial teaching, the most gigantic construction of spiritual precepts—the ritual formation of Judaism ; and that tradition of religious science which is second only to gnosis in image-making power, and superior to it in systematisation—the Kabbalah.

The two traditions were naturally in personal union with each other in the kabbalists, but they did not experience the full union of one reality of life and community, until they were taken up into Chassidism.

The union was brought about through the old/new principle which Chassidism presented, the principle of man's responsibility for God's fate in the world. Responsibility not in a conditioned, moral sense, but in an unconditioned, metaphysical sense, the secret, unfathomable value of human action, the influence of the man who acts on the history of the All, yes even on the powers that determine it—that is an *ur*-old conception in Judaism. 'The righteous enlarge the power of the upper dominion'. There is a causality of action which is withdrawn from our experience, and which is only open to our dimmest forefeeling.

Through the kabbalistic view of God's fate in the world this conception crystallised itself in the development of the Kabbalah into the central and bearing idea of Chassidism.

Mythically active in its operation in Iranian religious feeling, outlined in abstract thought in diverse kinds of gnosis, we perceive the conception of the soul of God emprisoned in the material world, from which it must be liberated. The glory of light which radiates from God and has sunk into darkness, the *sophia* which has been delivered into the hands of the lower powers that rule the world, the 'Mother' who must walk through all the sufferings of all existence—it is always the fate of a being mediating between original good and original evil which is told, a being who is delivered up and yet a being who is divine, severed from its origin and yet not severed from it ; for the severance is called time, and the union eternity. The Kabbalah has taken over the conception of the chained soul of God, but it has recast it in the fire of the Jewish conception of unity, which excludes any original duality. The

fate of God's glory, of ' the indwelling ', the
shekhinah, does not any longer come upon her
from her antithesis, not from the power of matter
alien or inimical to God, but from the necessity of
the original will itself ; it belongs to the meaning
of the creation.

How is world possible ? That is the essential
question for Kabbalah, as it was the essential
question for all gnosis. How can world be,
seeing that God is ? Seeing that God is infinite,
how can there be anything outside him ? Seeing
that he is eternal, how can time endure ?
Seeing that he is perfect, how could imperfection
arise ? Seeing that he is unconditioned, what has
the conditioned to do ?

The Kabbalah* answers : God contracted himself into world, because he who was the unity free
from all duality and relations would let relations
emerge ; because he would be known, loved,
willed ; because from his original oneness, in which
thought and its object are one, he would let the
otherness emanate, which strives towards unity.
So the spheres radiated from him, the spheres of
differentiation, creation, formation, action ; the
worlds of ideas, of powers, of form, of matter ; the
kingdoms of genius, of spirit, of soul, of life ; so
was formed in them the All, whose ' place ' God is,
and whose centre is he. The meaning of the emanation is according to a chassidic saying ' not, as
the creatures wrongly think, that the upper world
should be above the lower world, rather is the world
of action that which appears to our corporeal eye ;
but if you fathom it more deeply, and if you unfold
its corporeality, then this is even the world of
formation, and do you unfold it further, then is it
the world of creation, and do you still more deeply

---

* I do not here consider the development and transformation of the
kabbalistic view, but only the essential part of it which was determining for Chassidism.

probe its nature, then is it the world of differentiation, until the unlimited, blessed be HE '.  The
sensual world of space and time is only the outermost veil of God, the outermost and thickest
' shell ', therefore also called above all others ' the
world of shells '.  There is no evil in itself ; the
imperfect is only clasp and cover of a more perfect.

By this is not meant, however, that all world-
existence is to be taken as mere appearance, but
that it is regarded as a system of ever thicker
covering.  And yet, it is just in this system that
the fate of God is completed.  God has not made a
universe that experiences a fate, while he himself
is without any fate ; in so far as he himself projected the universe out of himself, he clad himself
in It, dwells in it, he himself in his shekhinah has
his own fate in the world.

But why were not the pure sphere of differentiation, and the world of ideas sufficient for the *ur*-will?
He who desired to be known could in these have
been known face to face.  Why had the first act
to produce beyond these worlds ever ' lower ',
ever more distant, outer, more shell-covered
domains, till it brought forth this world which
cannot be more thickly covered than it is, this
stubborn, troubled, burdened world in which we
creatures, we things, have our dwelling ?  Why
could we not remain genius, as light as the ether,
why had we successively to be stained and inter-
penetrated by a spirit of fire, a soul of water, an
earthy, corporeal life ?

To all such questions the Kabbalah answers
only :  God contracted himself into the world.
And it is answered.  God would be known, loved,
willed ;  that is, God wanted an independent
otherness, which would be free in its knowing, free
in its loving, free in its willing ; *he set it free*.  This
is the meaning of *zimzum*, contraction.  But as
this otherness was a power exempted from eternal

being, and which was given its freedom, it was only
limited in its freedom by its own doing ; it surged
forth beyond its godlike purity. Becoming burst
forth out of being, what the Kabbalah calls ' the
Mystery of the Splintering of the Vessels ' took
place. Sphere mounted out of sphere, world
climbed away beyond world, shell shot from shell,
till the limit of transformations was reached ; here
in the kingdom of matter extended in space, existing in time, on the edge of that which has become,
in the uttermost border-land of sensual things,
breaks the wave of God. The wave which breaks
here is God's. As the light precipitated itself
from the highest to the lowest spheres and shattered
them, the sparks of light from the *ur*-being who
lives in the immediate presence of God, from the
genius-natured Adam Kadmon, sink into the em-
prisonment of things. God's shekhinah descended
from sphere to sphere, wandered from world to
world, enveloped itself with shell upon shell,
until it was in its furthest exile—us. In our world
is God's fate fulfilled.


But our world is indeed the world of men.

In ancient Indian religion we meet the myth of
' The First Offer ', the sacrifice of the *ur*-man out
of whose parts the world has been created. The
idea of the *ur*-being, of human kind, who must
perish or humiliate himself that the separation of
the world may be accomplished, returns again and
again in the mystery-rites and cult-hymns, cos-
mogonies and apocalypses of the Near East. The
Kabbalah posits at the beginning of creation the
Adam Kadmon, the body of God, and the *ur*-image
of the All, God's light his substance, God's name
his life, the still brooding elements of the spheres
his members, all contraries in him connected as
right and left. The sundering of his parts is the

becoming of the world ; also this is sacrifice. But at their end, on the edge of that which has come into being, the effect of all the breaking and turmoil of the *ur*-light, the usury of all the spheres, all contraries fallen apart in him into male and female, stands again man, the combined work of the elements, this earthly, singled-out, called, metabolically changing, countlessly born and dead man. The otherness left to its freedom has worked itself out in him to its last drop, it has gathered itself in him, and he, the latest, most burdened, of created things has above them all received the full heritage of freedom. Here only, in this child of corruption and light, has the rightful subject of the first act arisen, he in whom God wills to be known, loved, willed. Here is the movement at an end, from this point only can ' the Jordan flow uphill '. Here the decision takes place. In other teachings the soul of God is sent from heaven to earth, or delivered over to the earth, and it can thus be called home or set free for its home, creation and redemption can take place from ' above ' to ' below ', in the same direction ; not so in a teaching which, like the Jewish teaching, is so completely established on the double-sided relationship between the I of man and the you of God, on the reality of the mutual relationship, on the *meeting*. Here is man, this miserable man, in accordance with the original intention of his creation, God's helper. The world was created for the sake of ' the chooser', for the sake of him who had the power to choose God. The shells of the world exist that he may break through them, into the centre. The spheres have bent apart that he might draw them together. The creature waits for him. God waits for him. The impulse to redemption must proceed from him, from ' below '. Grace is God's *answer*.

None of the upper, inner worlds are fit to give the first impulse to the transformation into the

*olam ha-tikkum,* the world of consummation, in
which ' the shekhinah steps out of the conceal-
ment', only this lowest and outermost world is fit
for that. For God has contracted himself to world,
he has set the world in freedom; fate hangs now on
the world's freedom. That is the *mysterium* of man.


The history of the world is repeated in the
history of man. That which has become free over-
reaches itself. To ' the Splintering of the Vessels '
corresponds ' the Fall of Man '. Both are signs
of the necessary way. Within the cosmic exile of
the shekhinah lies the earthly exile, into which it
was driven by the failure of man, and together
with him it goes out from Paradise into wandering
and error. The history of the world repeats itself
yet once more in the history of Israel. Banishment follows time and again on Israel's falling
away, not as a punishment, but as an effect ; and
the shekhinah goes into banishment with Israel,
until the last, where now, in deepest humiliation,
' all depends on turning'.

The Kabbalah completed this association of a
cosmic conception with a historical conception from
old Jewish traditions, and it certainly was conducive
in making the standpoint of the emanational systems
more immediately and easily accessible ; but at the
same time the meaning and task of man became
straitened. By confusing absolute and historical
categories all eschatology is always in danger of
sacrificing the eternal to the temporal ; this happens
all the more easily in an age where thought construction takes the place of eschatological vision.
The goal is made finite, and so the means is made
finite. If the inwardness of messianism, of the
world's turning and the world's transformation,
is forgotten, then a theurgical practice easily arises,
which wants to bring about redemption by statutory

procedures. This practice soars above itself on the mighty arches resting heavily on nought, which bring it to asceticism; this is what marked the last, pre-chassidic phase of the Kabbalah, and whose after-effects stretched into Chassidism itself, but which was overcome by the latter's anti-ascetical tendency. In most cases a small scheme of redemption will be left to stand over against the great cosmogonic vision of world-embracing *ur*-men.

In connection with the Kabbalah Chassidism strove to eradicate the schematisation of the *mysterium*. The old/new' principle which it represented is the principle of the cosmic and meta-cosmic power and responsibility of man, which it brought forth again in a purified form. ' All worlds hang on his works, all worlds look and yearn for the teaching and good deeds of man '. Owing to the sheer intensity with which it held this principle, Chassidism became a religious *movement* ; but the principle is no new teaching, and Chassidism does not either contain any new elements of teaching. Through the suppression, but not extinction, of the multitudinous forces of violence, formels of faith, and mystosofisms which clung to it, this principle became the centre of a mode of living and of a community. The eschatological urge did not die out, the demand for the messianic redemption found sometimes a still more personal expression in magic-compelling words and stormy enterprises ; but the work for the sake of the end— which an old saying bids us ' not to hurry '—subordinated itself to the steady working on the inner world through the hallowing of all acts ; in the stillness the conception ripened of a timeless salvation, which the moment discloses ; the decisive factor was no longer act, but the consecration of all acts ; and as the secret of present fulfilment united itself with the secret of preparing for things to come, and thus made it stronger and more illuminating, from out of asceticism, as from out of a sloughed off chrysalis cocoon, fluttered the winged joy.

Chassidism wants to reveal ' the God in this nethermost, lowest world, in all things, and specially in man, that there is no part and no movement of his in which the strength of God is not concealed, and none with which he cannot complete the unification '. To the question of what service should come first Baalshem answered, ' For the spiritual men the first service is, love without penance ; for others, to learn to see that there is a holy life in everything corporeal, and that one can carry back all to this root, and hallow all.'

There is no reason to fast, as he who eats with devotion redeems the fallen sparks enclosed in the food, and gives them smell and taste ; even Haman was affected by the holiness of the meal, when he was Esther's guest, and it is said about Abraham that he stood ' over ' the angels he gave food and drink, because he showed them the consecration of eating, which was unknown to them. There is no reason to do without love of husband or wife, for where a man and woman are together in holy unity, there the shekhinah rests over them—as already the Talmud taught. After the death of his wife Baalshem would not allow himself to be comforted, and said, ' I had hoped to journey to heaven in a thunderstorm like Elijah, but now it has been taken from me, for now I am after all only the half of one body '. One shall not undertake penances ; ' he who does harm to his body does harm to his soul ', and ecstasy arising from ascetical practices comes ' from the other side ' ; they are not of divine but of demonic, character. One shall not kill ' the evil drive ', the passion, in oneself, but one shall serve God *with it* ; it is the power which is destined to receive its direction from man. ' You have made the drive evil ', says God already in the Midrash to man ; the ' alien thoughts ', the lust which come to men, are pure ideas which were

made corrupt in ' the Splintering of the Vessels ',
and which now desire to be raised up again through
man. ' Though the noblest of bitterness still
touches despair, yet the lowliest of joys grows out
of holiness '. One cannot reach the kernel of the
fruit except through the shell. A zaddik[1] quoted
the word of a talmudic sage, ' The ways on the
firmament are as light to me as the ways of the
town of Nehardea ', and turned it round, ' The
streets of the town should be as light to one as the
paths of heaven ; for '' one cannot come to God
in any other way than through nature '' '.


'Enoch was a cobbler ; with each stitch of his
awl that drew together the top and bottom leather,
he joined God and his shekhinah'. Chassidic
teaching loved to vary this strange contribution to
the legend of the *ur*-father, who was favoured with
divine companionship, and was taken away from
this earth to undergo the transformation into
Metatron with his demiurgic powers, the fire-
bodied ' Prince of the Countenance '. For the
legend expresses by its image, which keeps so close
to the earth, what is the essential point to Chassidism, that man exerts influence on the eternal, and
that this is not done by any special works, but by
the intention with which he does all his works.
It is the teaching of the hallowing of the everyday.
The issue is not to attain to a new type of acting
which, owing to its object, would be sacred or
mystical ; the issue is to do the one appointed task,
the common, obvious tasks of daily life, according
to their truth and according to their meaning. Also
one's works are shells ; he who finishes his work
rightly, hallowing it, encompasses the limitless in
its core.

From this it becomes clear that Chassidism
had no impulse to tear out any part of the structure
of traditional Law, for, according to chassidic teach-

ing, nothing can exist which cannot be filled with intention, or whose intention cannot be discovered. But it also becomes clear how just by this the force of inertia secretly remained stronger than the moving and renewing force, and finally inside Chassidism itself necessarily overcame it; it is only the old story that in the world of men the shell ever prevails over the kernel.

Even apart from that, no teaching finds it so hard to preserve its pure strength as one which places the meaning of life in the effective reality of the here and now, and which does not suffer men to seek refuge from the exacting infinity of the moment in an equally accepted system of being and of being commanded; the force of inertia always proves itself the stronger, and compels the teaching to recant. But during the short time of its purity the teaching has begotten an undying fullness of the true and generous life.

# Body

A teaching which sets the winged How of an act high above the codified What is not able to hand down its substance in writing; it is again and again transmitted by life, from leader to followers, but especially from master to disciple. It is not as if the teaching were divided into one part which was open to all, and into another part of esoteric teaching; it would go against its own purpose, the work on humanity, if it harboured a secret chancellery with a hieratic inscription above its door. It is rather that while the secret which is handed down is exactly the same as that which the enduring word proclaims, its nature as a How prevents it from being more than indicated by the word; the substance of its truth is only open to him who verifies it by his life.

Hence ' a hidden zaddik ' said about the rabbis

who ' speak Torah ', that is, who interpreted the
Scriptures, ' What is the sense of their speaking
Torah ? Man should act in such a way that all his
behaviour is a Torah, and he himself is a Torah '.
And at another time it is said, ' The aim of the wise
man is to make himself into a perfect teaching, and
all his acts bodies of instruction ; and where it is
not vouchsafed him to attain to this, his aim is to
be a transmission of the teaching and a commentary
on it, and to spread the teaching by each of his
movements '. It comes as a sacramental expression
of this fundamental insight when the Zaddik of
Apt picks up the belt which the seventeen year old
Rabbi Israel, the later Riziner, had dropped,
buckles it on for him saying that he completes the
holy act of the gelilah,² the rolling up of the Torah-
scroll.

The men in whom the Torah-nature fulfils
itself are called zaddiks, ' the righteous ', the lawful.
They are the bearers of chassidic teaching, not only
as its apostles, but more as its effective reality.
They are the teaching.

In order to understand the particular significance of the zaddik, as distinct for instance from
that of the Russian staretz as he has been presented
with the illuminating fidelity of a great poet, by
Dostojewski, it is necessary to remember the
fundamental difference between the historical conceptions of Judaism and Christianity, or one of
the other religions centering in a saviour, such as
Buddhism for example. It is not the conception
of redemption itself which is the dividing factor ;
that existed already in the messianism of the
prophets, and post-exiletic Judaism elaborated it
as the central theme of its conception of the world.
But in the saviour religions the redemption is a
fact which, even while it transcends history, as it
must according to its nature, yet also is a fixed point
localised in history ; for Judaism redemption is

not a fact, but pure futurity. For Christianity historical time, ' the present aeon ', has a caesura, an absolute middle-point, where it, as it were, breaks open so violently that it becomes split from top to bottom, and just by doing this it obtains its unshakable hold. For Judaism, on the other hand, historical time must run to its ' end ' without such a central mooring point, completely left to its never-ceasing flowing. Finality has in this way intervened in Christianity, as in Buddhism, and it can from now on only be ' imitated ', only be renewed by annexation, only be re-enacted. In Judaism finality intervenes at all times, that is, it intervenes here and now. Before the glowing plenitude of fate given by the here and now even the horizon of ' the last things ' is apparently drained of its colour before our eyes; the Kingdom of God projected on to time appears on the horizon of the absolute future, where heaven and earth meet ; but timelessly it reveals itself ever and again in the moment where truly human beings act with the whole of their nature, and thus unite God and his shekhinah. It is true it was a Christian, European man of vision who confronted his Church with the statement, ' The noble man is that only-begotten son of God whom the Father eternally bears '*; but in none of the Christian heretical communities which wanted to be in earnest with this point of view could it grow into an unequivocal life. In Chassidism arose the parallel saying of Judaism, weak and condemned to distortion from its beginning, but enduring in its reality, in which the place of ' conception ' is taken by the never-ceasing stream of the down-flowing grace, by the meeting of divine and human work, but where through the human work the ' eternal ' rings with equal strength.

---

* One of the propositions of Eckhardt's which was condemned by the Pope in 1329.

The zaddik is neither a priest nor a monk, who
renews in himself an act of salvation finished once
and for all, or who mediates this act of salvation to
the community ; the zaddik is the man who is more
intent than other men on putting his hand to the
task of salvation, which is common to all human
beings and all times, whose powers purified and
united are turned to the one duty. He is, according to the conception of him, the man in whom
the metaphysical responsibility of human beings
steps out from its preceding existence as a conception in the consciousness of mankind, and takes
on organic existence. He is the man who has
become truly human, the rightful subject of the
act in which God wills to be known, loved, willed.
In him the ' lower ', earthly man makes real and
actual his *ur*-image, becomes the cosmic *ur*-man
who encompasses the spheres. He is the turning
of the great flood, in him the world turns back
towards its fountain-head. He is ' no servant of
time, but above her '. He carries the blessing from
below to the upper realms, and the upper blessing
to the lower realms ; he draws the Holy Ghost
down over mankind. The existence of the zaddik
has its influence also in the upper realms. As one
zaddik said about another in a joking way which is
as hearty as it is clear, ' He must boil huge pots at
his fire '. From him does the world take its
renewal, he is its ' foundation ' ; this is the interpretation given of Solomon's saying about ' the
righteous ' in *Proverbs*, 10.25, ' The zaddik is
called foundation, because he ceaselessly causes
the outpouring of abundance over the world with
his work. And if it fulfils itself from him so that
the aim of all his acts is now only to unite God with
his shekhinah, then a stream of grace comes over
his soul from the divine abundance which flows
from the light of the One God, and he becomes like
a new creature, and like a newborn babe. This is

what is written, " Unto Shem, also was born he
. . ."* For he whose every work is for God, he
conceives himself in the renewal of the light in his
soul '.

A truly human being is of more importance than
an angel, as the angel is ' one who stands ', but he
is ' one who walks '; he walks on, penetrates
through, ascends up—he completes the decisive,
renewing movement of the world. The constant
renewal is the guiding principle of the zaddik's
life. In him the preceding becoming of creation
gathers itself and raises itself to its creative meaning,
the true one which is quite free from self-will and
self-seeking, which indeed is nothing less than the
turning back of creation to its creator. The zaddik
sees continually the bodily renewal immediately
in the all, and is ' in each moment moved by the
renewal of the creature '; his nature answers with
the renewal of the spirit. And as the bodily
renewal in nature is always connected with a sub-
mersion, a dissolution, a sleep of the elements, so
there is no true spiritual becoming without extinction. ' For the zaddikim ', says Rabbi Sussja,
' who in their service ever go from temple to temple,
and from world to world, must first of all throw
their life from them that they may receive a new
spirit, so that a new inspiration ever can overshadow
them ; and this is the mystery of sleep '. The
symbolic act of this deeply inward event is the
immersion. Primeval symbol of re-birth, which is
only genuine when it includes death and resurrection, it was taken up into kabbalistic practice from
old traditions, especially from those of the Essenes
and the 'morning baptisers ', and was practised by
the zaddikim with a profound and joyful eagerness
which has no asceticism in it. It is told of many of
the zaddikim how they broke the ice on the streams

---

* Interpreting the translation of *Genesis*, 10. 21.

in the heavy winter-frosts to be able to immerse themselves in running water ; the meaning of this fervour is shown by the words of a chassid who said that the spiritual act of ' the laying aside of all bodyliness ' could be substituted for immersion. What here finds expression by the action is readiness and preparedness to enter into ' the state of nothing ' in which alone the divine renewal can work itself out.

In this ever new exercise of ' the receptive power ' of the zaddik is completed the ever new consecration of his active power. Armed with renewed strength he returns again to his work— his daily work, to the myriad-sided work of ' unification ', of the *jichud*.

Jichud means primarily the proclamation of the unity of God, which is for the Jews the central sun not only in their religious system, but also in the whole system of their lives. This proclamation represents, however, not a passive acknowledgement, but an act. It is in no way the statement of a subject about an object ; it is not at all anything ' subjective ', it is something subjective-objective, it is the one act of meeting, it is the dynamic form of the divine unity itself. This active character of the jichud grew in strength in the Kabbalah, and came to its own in Chassidism. Man produces the unity of God ; this means that the unity of becoming, God's unity in creation, completes itself through him ; according to its nature this unity can admittedly only be a unification of that which has separated itself originally, a unification which bridges the lasting state of separation, and in which the original unity of the undivided being finds its cosmic counterpart : The unity without multiplicity in the unification of multiplicity.

It is of basic importance to contrast the characteristic conception of the jichud with magic

action. The magic act implies the influence of a
subject on an object, that of the man versed in
magic on a power that may be divine or demonic,
personal or impersonal, appearing in the world of
things or hiding behind it ; hence it implies a
constitutive duality of elements in which the one
element, the human, is essentially the weaker, but
in virtue of its magic power it becomes the stronger
element which can exert compulsion on the other ;
it forces the other element, be this divine or
demonic, to serve man, to fulfil man's purpose, to
work for man ; man, from whom the act springs,
is also its goal and end ; the magic act forms a
causal process which is isolated, circular, and turns
back into itself. The jichud does not imply the
influence of a subject on an object, but rather that
something objective works itself out in and through
something subjective, being works itself out in and
through becoming. This is a true, strict, and
complete working out, so that the becoming is not
a tool that is being moved hither and thither, but a
mover which is released, free, working in its own
freedom. World history is not a game played by
God ; it is God's fate. The jichud means the
ever-new binding together of the spheres that
strive to be apart, the ever-new betrothal of
' majesty ' and ' kingdom '—through man. The
divine element which lives in man moves from him
to serve God, to do God's purpose, to work for
God. The free jichud is done in God's name and
in accordance with his command when he created
the world, and he himself is its goal and end ; the
jichud does not turn back into itself, it turns
back into God ; it is not isolated, but is interwoven
with the world process ; it is no circle, but the
swing back of the power of God which he sent
forth.

From this distinction between them it is clear
why magic must include a qualitatively particular

action which has to bring forth the particular effect, why it must include gestures and speeches of a particular kind, alien to other men and other moments, while jichud, on the other hand, has no special formula and procedure, but, on the contrary, is nothing ·else than the ordinary life of human beings, only gathered together and directed towards its goal of union. It is true that Chassidism has taken up and practised much of kabbalistic tradition, such as the secret of the letters of the alphabet, the twisting round and joining together of the names of God in its system of ' kawanoth ',[3] of meditations ; but this magical part has never touched the centre of chassidic teaching. In this centre there is no secret formula, but the hallowing of everything ; nothing which is done can be condemned to remain profane on account of its nature ; each act becomes divine service and divine work when it is directed towards the union, that is, when the union becomes revealed in its inner consecration. The life of the zaddik is carried by this all-penetrating power of the jichud.

It is told of the Zaddik of Berditschew that while he was still young he was once staying with his friend, the Rabbi of Mikulov, and that while he was staying with him, he caused general offence, because he went ·into the kitchen dressed in his prayer shawl and with the double phylacteries on his forehead, and asked after the preparation of the food ; and also because he would enter into talk with the most worldly man about all kinds of apparently idle things, even in the house of prayer ; that was profanation of the sacred garments, profanation of the sacred place, profanation of the sacred hour, and it was as such thrown up against him. But the Master said, ' What it is only in my power to do for three hours during the day, this man is able to do all day long, he can keep his mind collected, so that he establishes the eminent union also with the talk that is counted for idle '. The central desire of the zaddik is to hallow that which is worldly. His meal is a sacrifice, his table an altar. All his ways lead to redemption. It is told about one zaddik that when he was young he went day in and day out round the villages and traded with the peasants ; and again and again when he came home and said the afternoon prayer, he felt that a blessed fire coursed through all his body ; he asked his elder brother, who was also his teacher, what that was, for he was afraid that it might emanate from that which is evil, and that his service was untrue ; his brother answered, ' When you walk across the fields with your mind pure and holy, then from all the stones, and all growing things, and all animals, the sparks of their soul come out and cling to you, and then they are purified and become a holy fire in you '.

This hallowing of the everyday stands above all magic : The prayerbook of Rabbi Jizchak Lurja, the master of the theurgical Kabbalah, was published in the days of Rabbi Pinchas of Korez; this prayerbook was entirely built on letter-kawanoth, and the disciples of the Zaddik asked for his permission to use it for their prayers ; but after some time they came back to him and complained that since they had begun to use the prayer-book, they had suffered a great loss in their sensitiveness to a strong life of prayer. Rabbi Pinchas answered them, ' You have enclosed all your strength and all the striving of your thoughts towards the goal in the kawanoth on the holy name and the letter monograms and have turned away from the essential thing, to make your heart whole and unite it with God; therefore have you lost the life and feeling of holiness'. All formulae and artifices are patchwork, the true union rises above them all. ' He who uses in his prayer all the kawanoth which he knows ', says Baalshem, ' he produces only that which he knows. But he who speaks the word in great collectedness, for him all kawanah enters of itself into each word'. What can be learnt does not matter ; what matters is the self-abandonment to that which is not known.

A zaddik said, ' Note well that the word Kabbalah comes from kabbel, to take up, and the word kawanah comes from kawen, to direct. For the ultimate meaning of all the wisdom of the Kabbalah is to take upon oneself the yoke of the Kingdom of God ; and all the skill of the kawanoth is to direct one's heart to God. When a man says, " God is mine and I am his " how is it that his soul does not part from his body ?' As soon as he had said this, he fell into a deep swoon, from which he was only called back with great difficulty.

Here it becomes clear that jichud means a venture, the one venture. The unification of God must happen in the world, man must produce the unification of God by unifying himself; what belongs to man, worldly welfare, understanding, life on this earth, must be ventured on the divine. This shows itself most powerfully in prayer. It is told of a zaddik that every day, before he went to the house of prayer, he arranged his home as if he were going to die. Another zaddik taught his disciples how they should pray, ' He who says the word " Lord " and at the same time also has in his mind to say the words " of the world ", that is no way of speaking. But while he says " Lord ", he should in his mind completely relinquish himself to the Lord, and then his soul will go out into the Lord, and he cannot any longer pronounce the word " world ", and he shall be satisfied that he can say " Lord ". This is the nature of prayer'.[4] Baalshem has likened the ecstatic movements of the chassid who prays with the whole of his body to the movements of a drowning man.

What was already told of individual masters of

the Talmud became also soon told of some of the
zaddikim ; it was told how the rapture of prayer
ruled their bodies mightily and carried them away
to movements which went far beyond what is
customary in the world of humanity. In such
moments there was round many of them a remote-
ness as that round a holy maniac. But all this is
only incidents happening on the doorstep, and not
what takes place in the hall ; it is the struggling
venture, and not the fulfilment. Rabbi Jehuda
Leib tells us how once in the bower at the time of
the Feast of Tabernacles he saw the great Zaddik
of Lublin move as if driven by a secret terror before
the benediction ; all the people gazed at it, and
were themselves thrown into quivering fear ; Rabbi
Jehuda Leib, however, remained sitting and waited
till the time of the benediction ; then he arose,
looked at the now motionless, uplifted Master, and
listened to the divine benediction ; thus had Moses
once not heeded the clap of thunder and the smok-
ing mountain round which the people stood
tremblingly, and had drawn near to the motionless
cloud.

The less premeditated the prayer is, the more
spontaneously it wells forth from the natural deep
in man, from the cosmic impulse of him who
carries the likeness of the sphere-encompassing
*ur*-man, so much the more real is it. It is emphasised about a disciple's disciple of the Zaddik
of Lublin, Rabbi Mendel of Kozk, that he prayed
without any effort and strain, as one who talks with
his companion, and yet was transformed after the
prayer as if he came out of another world, and
scarcely recognised his own ; 'for the nature of
the talk issues from the root of the soul without any
intention ; like one whose soul is occupied with a
very profound subject sometimes lets words come
out of his mouth which are spoken between him and
himself without any intention, and he himself

knows nothing of his speech, and all this, because
it issues from the root of the soul, and the whole
soul is enwrapped in the speech, which rises in
perfect unity.'  Here, in true prayer, appears the
*ur*-meaning of the jichud in its purest form, and
shows that it is no ' subjective ' event, but that it
is the dynamic form of the very unity of God.
' The people think ', said Rabbi Pinchas of Korez,
' that they pray before God.  But it is not so with
them.  For the prayer itself is the essence of the
Godhood '.


Of this kind is the lonely service of the zaddik.
But he is not a true zaddik, who remains satisfied
with this.  The bond of God and man preserves
and fulfils itself in the world of man.

Rabbi Chajim of Zans was once after the
minchah[5] prayer troubled by an importunate person
with a certain request.  As the man would not
desist, the Zaddik became rude to him.  When
he was asked by a friend, who was present at the
scene, why he had been in such a rage, he answered
that he who says minchah stands face to face with
the world of the original severance, how should he
not be angry when he comes from this, and then
becomes besieged with the small troubles of the
small people.  To that the other said, ' After
Scripture has told of the first revelation of God on
Sinai to Moses, it says, " Moses went down from
the mount to the people ".  Rashi comments on
this, " This teaches us that Moses from the
mountain did not turn to his business, but to the
people ".  How is this to be understood ?  What
kind of business had Moses in the desert from which
he desisted in order to go to the people ?  But it is
to be understood thus: As Moses descended the
mountain, he still cleaved to the upper worlds and
completed his great work on them, interpenetrating

the sphere of judgement with the element of mercy.
This was Moses's business. And yet, as he stepped
down to the people, he ceased from his great work,
made himself free from the upper worlds and
turned himself to the people ; he listened to all their
small troubles, laid all the heaviness of the hearts
of all Israel on his own, and then he carried it up
in prayer " '. When Rabbi Chajim heard this,
his mind became calm and clear, he called the man
to whom he had spoken so harshly back again so
that he might be appraised of his request, and almost
throughout the whole night he received the com-
plaints and petitions of the chassidim gathered
there.

'Upper' and 'lower'—the determining importance belongs to the 'lower'. Here on the
edge of that which has come into being is the fate
of the aeons decided. The world of man is the
world of testing.

'Be, not bad with yourself', that means, do not
think that you cannot be redeemed, it is written in
*The Sayings of the Fathers*. But Rabbi Baruch,
the grandson of Baalshem, interpreted the saying
differently, 'Each man is called to bring something
in the world to its completion. Each one is needed
by the world. But there are people who always sit
and learn, shut into their rooms, and who do not
go out of the house to talk with other people ; for
this reason they are called bad people. For if they
talked with the others, they would bring something
of that which was appointed for them to completion. This is what it means, " be not bad with
yourself " ; what is meant is that you spend your
time sitting alone with yourself and do not go out
among the ·people ; be not bad through lone-
liness '.

Human love is not the fulfilment of a commandment coming from outside this world ; it is
work on the completion, it helps to bring the form

of the shekhinah out of its hiddenness, it works
on the ' chariot ', on the cosmic bearer of the
liberated glory.   It is written of this, ' Love your
neighbour as thyself, *I am he who is there* '.   On
love does the Kingdom establish itself.

' When a ' man sees that his neighbour hates
him ', said Rabbi Rafael of Berschad, ' then he
must love him more than he did before to fill up
what is lacking.   For the unity of love of all people
is the chariot of the shekhinah, and each jolt and
crack in it hinders its rise from out of the shells '.
Therefore Rabbi Rafael used always to warn
against applying the measuring-rod in one's dealings with people :  A surplus of love is necessary
to fill up what is lacking of love in this world.


There are three circles on which the love of the
zaddik is proved.
The first and widest circle includes all the many
people who come from afar to the zaddik ;  they
come most often at the time of the high holydays,
partly to spend some days near the zaddik, ' in the
shadow of his holiness ', partly to obtain help from
him in their distress of body or soul.   In these
pilgrims there is something of the same loyal and
trustful spirit as that with which the people of
Palestine once used to go up to the Temple in
Jerusalem three times a year to offer their sacrifice
in order to free themselves from evil and to join
themselves to the divine; 'the Zaddik takes the
place of the altar '.   It must be admitted that the
slips of paper with requests, which the travellers
handed in, contain mostly a list of quite exterior
wants and physical illnesses ;  but their healing
stirs the innermost depths and calls the people
back to themselves to begin a new life.   The two
conceptions of ' wonder ' and ' suggestion ' go
only a very little way towards helping us to under-

stand the general character of the phenomenon
which underlies this peculiar effect the zaddik had,
an effect whose existence cannot be contested.
' Wonder ' makes the irrationality of the phenomenon vanish into thin air, ' suggestion ' makes
its rationalisation fall flat on the earth ; to try to
pronounce it to be an influence of the divine on
the human gives a much too vague point of view,
as it would give a much too narrow point of view to
pronounce it to be an influence of the ' stronger '
will on the ' weaker ' will.   One may perhaps get
a right perspective to begin with, if one remembers
that the relation of a soul to its organic life depends
on the degree of wholeness and unity attained by
the soul; the more dissociated the soul is, so much the
more is it at the mercy of the organic life ; the more
unified it is in itself so much the more is it the
master of its physical illness and attacks from the
body ;   not as if it vanquished the body, but
because through its unity it ever saves and guards
the unity of the body.   Suddenly and unmistakably does this power rule where a shattered
soul in a supreme moment is gathered together
and is made whole.   The ' healing ', which hitherto
has grown only in the fruitful darkness of the depth
of the soul, is suddenly completed in the sight of
all.   Through nothing else can this process be
effected so simply and immediately as through the
psycho-synthetic appearance of a whole, unified
soul, which lays hold of the shattered soul, agitates
it on all sides, and hastens the event of crystallisa-
tion.   The unified soul does not use suggestion,
she shapes a resting-place and a centre in the soul
which has called out to her ; and she does this the
more truly and perfectly the more she takes care
that the soul which has called out to her does not
remain dependent upon her.   The helper establishes a resting-place and a centre not in so far as
he places his own image in the soul which has to

be formed anew, but in so far as he lets her see through him, as through a glass, the essence of all things, and then lets her uncover that essence in herself, and lets her appropriate it as the core of the living unity. Only the greatest among the zaddikim have accomplished this task ; they stand in the tradition of helpers of God.

The second, middle, circle includes those who live in the neighbourhood of the zaddik. These present usually only a part of the Jews of the neighbourhood, the rest are 'adversaries', *mitnagdim*, and those who are indifferent ; their official, spiritual leader is the ' rav ' ; within this group, as in ' a compulsory community ', stands the chassidic group as a free group, ' a community of choice ', with the zaddik, the ' rebbe ' at its head, although some zaddikim,. who lived in a place where Chassidism prevailed, also exercised the functions of the rav, and carried his title. This difference between the two groups shows the difference in the legal status of the rav and the rebbe. The rav qualified for his position by his proved knowledge of the Law in its talmudic roots, and in the whole fullness of its rabbinic ramifications ; the rebbe, on the other hand, qualified for his position by his spontaneously acknowledged leadership of souls, the depth of his ' fear of God', that is, the central feeling of God's presence, and the fervour of his ' heart's service ', that is the shaping of his whole life into an active prayer. By this, however, is by no means to be understood that the latter group of characteristics was only to be found among the zaddikim, and not also among the rabbis, just as little as it can be taken that many of the zaddikim had not an extensive and independently constructive knowledge of halakhah (Law). The greatest of the opponents of Chassidism, Rabbi Elijahu of Wilna, the ' Gaon ', was an exponent of the book *Zohar*, the cornerstone of the Kabbalah, and the greatest systematiser of Chassidism, Rabbi Schnëur Salman, the ' Rav of Reussen ', was the author of a codex of ritual laws ; and when one puts side by side the two life-histories as they have come down to us, then it is not the second but the first which has the mystical-legendary character. One must guard oneself against taking the antithesis, which inevitably arises in any consideration of the inner history of the two groups, in a pragmatic instead of in a dialectic sense ; the movement of the spirit fulfils itself in contradiction, but it does not embody itself in it. With this qualification the chassidic community can be considered as the social pre-sentation of the principle of voluntarism, and the zaddik as representing autonomous leadership. The strongest manifestation of both, and of their unity, is the common prayer ; it is the ever return-ing, yet ever new symbolic act of the union between the zaddik and the community. The oppressive, crowded room of the beth ha-midrash,* where overnight the poor travellers sleep, and where in the early morning the keen Talmud disputations resound, breathes now the air of the *mysterium*. Even in the places where the zaddik prays in a separate room is he united with his community into a corporate body.

The third and narrowest circle consists of the disciples, of whom some were usually taken into the household of the zaddik. This is the real place of tradition, the imparting of the teaching from generation to generation.

Each of the three circles has its unity in virtue of the interaction between it and the zaddik. About ' the travellers ' Rabbi Pinchas says, ' Often when some one comes to me to ask advice, I hear how he gives himself the answer '. Baalshem has

---

* Common prayer-house and school.

likened the community, especially at prayer, to a bird's nest which one sets several people to get from the top of a very tall tree ; one person is placed standing on the shoulders of the one below, he himself stands topmost ; and what would happen if even one of the human pillar thought that it took too long to get the nest ! But the power of interaction is most fully shown in the third circle.

In a town not far from that in which Rabbi Nachum of Tschernobil lived, some of his disciples were once sitting at ' the farewell meal of the Queen ', which once more gathers the devout together before the Sabbath is ushered out ; and as they were sitting, they spoke of the account which the soul has to give of itself in its deepest self-reflection. Then it came over them in their fear and humility that it seemed to them as if the life of them all were thrown away and squandered, and they said to each other that there would be no hope for them any more were it not that it comforted them and gave them confidence that they were allowed to join themselves to the great zaddik, Rabbi Nachum. Then they all rose, driven by a common desire, and set forth on the way to Tschernobil. At the same time as this was happening, Rabbi Nachum was sitting in his house, giving account of his soul. Then it seemed also to him in his fear and humility as if his life were thrown away and squandered, and that all his confidence came from only this one thing that these God-drunken men had joined themselves to him. He went to the door, and looked towards the dwelling-place of the disciples ; and when he had been standing there for a time, he saw them coming. ' In this moment ', added the zaddik, when he told of the event, ' did the ring snap fast '.

As here the mutual value for each other finds its expression, so we see in another story the mutual influence expressed : On one of the days of self-examination between the New Year and the Day of Atonement Rabbi Sussja was sitting in his chair, and the chassidim stood round him from morning till night. He had raised heart and eye to heaven, and released himself from all corporeal bonds. Looking at him awoke in one of the disciples the desire for repentance, and he began to weep profusely ; and as a live coal makes its neighbours begin to kindle, so the flame of repentance alighted on disciple after disciple. Then the Zaddik looked round and looked at them all. Again he lifted his eyes, and spoke to God, saying, ' Truly, Lord of the world, it is the right time to repent before you ; but you know well that I have not the strength to do penance—therefore accept my love and my shame as penance.' It is this kind of influence which I have pointed to as that handing on of the secret which is above words.

Again and again it says in the chassidic writings that one should learn ' from all the members of the zaddik'. The purifying and renewing influence comes above all from the spontaneity of his existence ; the consciously thought out utterances, especially those in verbal form, are only an accompaniment. The essence of spontaneity is also the determining factor in the verbal utterances.

' Make me a place of offering from the earth of the field . . . ' it says in Scripture, ' but if you make me a place of offering of stone, build it not of fashioned stone, for if you have swung your iron over it, then you have given it up '. The altar of earth, thus the Riziner expounds, that is the one which pleases God above all, the altar of silence ; if, however, you make your altar out of words, then do not fashion them'.

The zaddik shuns ' the beautiful ', the premeditated human speech. A learned man who was once a Sabbath-day guest at the table of Rabbi

Baruch said to him, ' Let us now hear words of teaching, you speak so beautifully '. ' Before I speak beautifully, may I become dumb ', said Baalshem's grandson. And said not another word.

At the holiest of the Sabbath-day meals, ' the third meal ', the zaddik expounds the teaching, mostly only sparingly and fitfully, again and again breaking it off with silence, wrapped in deep meditation ; a soft song, woven of the secret, goes before, an enraptured anthem follows. As often as the silence enters the darkening room, it brings an echo of eternity.

The three circles on which the love of the zaddik is tested, the coming and going crowd of those who seek his help, the community which is bound together by place and living conditions, the strong ring of souls formed by the disciples, all these indicate the various moving forces of which the vitality of the chassidic movement was built up. Its spiritual structure was founded on the handing down of the core of the teaching from master to disciple, but not as if something was transmitted to them which was not also open to all ; only, in the presence of the master, in the natural working of his being, the inexpressible How fluttered free and descended on them, bearing its fruit. But even the same thing, only in an uncondensed and confused form was imparted to the people in the words of advice and teaching, and was developed in the customs and brotherly life of the community. This absence of grading in its province of teaching, this its anti-hierarchical position secured Chassidism its power over the people. It did not take away from outside the prime of place given to possessions, but made them of no value from inside by linking together rich and poor in a community of mutual material and spiritual help, a community

of love, in which all members are equal before God
and the zaddik ; in the same way it also overcame,
and in its highest moments fully overcame, the far
stronger, and in Judaism *ur*-stronger, precedence
given to learning, to talmudic as well as to kabbalistic learning. The ' spiritual ' man, the man
who works with his brain, is not as such nearer the
divine, indeed so long as he does not unify the
manifoldness of his life, which lends itself to
different interpretations, and so long as he has not
subdued the violence of his labour to calmness,
he may be further from the divine than ' the simple
man ', who was already despised in the talmudic era,
the ' am ha-aretz ' (countryman), who with peasant
trustfulness leaves his cause to heaven.

The combination of purity of teaching and
heritage of the people is made possible by the
fundamental principle of the chassidic teaching,
the hallowing of all that belongs to this world.
There is within this world no gulf between higher
and lower human beings ; to each is the highest
open, each life has its entrance to reality, each kind
of man has his eternal right, from each thing does a
way lead to God, and each way that leads to God
is *the* way.

So long as the combination of purity of teaching
and being a heritage of the people, of immediate
transmission and a structure open to all, lasted,
Chassidism was full of light and fruitful. Their
disintegration meant its dissolution.

## Spinoza, Sabbatai Zwi, and Baalshem

Twenty-three years before Baalshem was born,
two famous Jews died within a short time of
each other ; both of them had ceased to be members of the Jewish community, the philosopher,
Baruch Spinoza, because he had been excom-
municated by the Synagogue, the ' Messiah',

Sabbatai Zwi, because he had seceded to Islam. Both of these men mark a late-exilitic catastrophe within Jewry ; the thought and writings of Spinoza bear witness to a spiritual upheaval and its influence on the Gentile world ; the work of Sabbatai Zwi shows a rupture within the life and inner structure of the community itself. Although from the point of view of history Spinoza has had no important influence on Jewry, he yet belongs essentially to this historical cycle. Just as Sabbatai Zwi's secession to Islam indicates a traditional doubt of the Jewish doctrine of the Messiah, so Spinoza's teaching voices a traditional doubt of the Jewish conception of God. Thus both men terminate a process which flowed from one historical event, namely, that of the appearance of Jesus ; and both men receive their answer and correction from a new process which sprang from one historical event, namely, that of the appearance of Baalshem.

The great achievement of Israel is not so much that it has told mankind of the one, real God, the origin and goal of all that exists, but rather that it has taught men that this God does in very reality hear when they speak to him, that men can be natural with him, that we human beings can stand face to face with him, that there is communion between God and man. It is true that wherever man is found, there prayer is also found, and so it has been from the dawn of time ; but it was only Israel who conceived life itself as a being spoken to and giving answer, a speaking to and receiving answer, and who lived out this conception in the actual terms of living. It is true that mystery cults have existed at all stages of human development, and that these cults have professed to lead men to communion with the deity ; but the more intimate the communion was said to be, the more it was a pretence. Here, as everywhere else where we are invited to participate in exceptional conditions and not in the lived life of the every day, we find that the God who is discovered is only the human image of a partial manifestation of the real God, he who is the origin and goal of all that exists :

> The little finger of his left hand
> Was called Pan

God, in all actual fact, as speaker, the creation as the language, the call into Nothing, and the answer of things through their emergence, the language of creation continued in the life of each created substance, the life of each creature a dialogue, the world the word—to proclaim that was left to Israel. Israel taught and showed : The real God is the God who can be spoken to, because he is the one who speaks to men.

Jesus—though not the actual man Jesus, but the picture of Jesus as it has arisen in the souls of men and changed them—leaves God to be approachable only in conjunction with himself, the Christ ; the human word can only penetrate to him who is the origin and goal of all being, when it is carried by him, the Logos ; the ' way ' to the Father is only through him. It was with this modification that the Gentiles received Israel's teaching about the approachable God. Thus it came about that they learned to speak not to God, but to Christ.

Spinoza undertook to rob God of his approachableness. By this is not to be understood that his *deus sive natura* was another God. He himself meant none other than the God to whom he had spoken when he was a boy, the same God who is the origin and goal of all that exists. Spinoza wanted only to purify him from the stain of being approachable. That which could be spoken to

was not pure, not great, not divine enough for
him. Spinoza's fundamental mistake was that he
imagined that the teaching of Israel included only
the teaching that God is a person ; and he turned
against this as a lessening of the Godhood. But
the truth of the teaching lies in its insistence that
God is *also* a person ; and that stands over against
all impersonal, unapproachable ' purity ' on the
part of God as a heightening of the Godhood.
Solomon, who built the Temple, knew that God
shows himself in light, but dwells in darkness,
that all the heavens cannot contain him, but that
yet he has chosen for himself a house among those
who speak to him ; that thus he is both person
and non-person, as much the limitless and the
nameless as the Father who has taught his children
to speak familiarly with him. Spinoza knows only
of the alternative, person or non-person ; he then
overthrows person, as if it were an idol, and
proclaims the uncreated substance with whom
it would be folly or lyricism to speak familiarly.

However little late-exilitic Jewry heard about
him, something from Jewry had been brought to
pass in the Gentile world, and what is brought
about cannot be separated from its origin. Through
Christianity, in however modified a form, something had penetrated into the Gentile world from
the innermost being of Israel ; it is extremely
significant that only a Jew could show how to take it
away again; a Jew had brought it about. Spinoza
helped the minds of the spiritual among the Gentiles to set themselves free from that which had been
grafted on to them. Spinoza decisively accelerated
the tendency of the Western mind to live a life of
soliloquy—and with that he precipitated the whole
spiritual crisis ; for the spirit withers in the air of
the triumphant monologue.

Presumably Baalshem knew nothing about
Spinoza ; but that does not prevent Baalshem from

giving him his answer. It is part of historical truth that a man can answer, though he has not heard ; he does not intend to give an answer by what he says, but it is an answer nevertheless. It does not make Baalshem's answer of less importance that it did not reach the minds of those who heard Spinoza's word ; for that which is unknown remains also of permanent value in historical truth.

In order to make clear how it comes about that the chassidic message has this character of answer, I shall have to refer to one of the fundamental tenets of Spinoza's teaching; a tenet which is closely associated with his attempt to ' purify ' God, although it seems to belong to a still deeper level of the soul than that from which ' purifying ' arises.

The real communion of man with God has not only its place in the world, but also its object. God speaks to man in the things and beings whom he sends him in life. Man answers through his dealings with these things and beings. All specific ' divine service ' is in itself only the ever-renewed preparation for and hallowing of this communion with God in the world. But it is the ancient danger, perhaps it is the most extreme danger and temptation of man, that something comes to be taken away and isolated from the human side ; what has been taken away then becomes independent, rounded off and completed till it looks as if it were interchangeable with the whole from which it sprang ; and then it is substituted for the real communion. The *ur*-danger of man is ' religion '. It may be the forms by which man hallows the world for God that become independent, what we may call the ' cult-sacramental ' forms ; then they cease to embody the consecration of the lived, everyday life, and become instead the means of its separation from God ; life

in the world and divine service run on unapproach-
ably parallel lines.  But the ' God ' of this divine
service is no longer God, it is the mask, the real
partner in the communion is no longer there, the
worshipper gesticulates into the empty air.  Or,
it may be the state of soul underlying the divine
service that becomes independent, the devotion,
the reaching-out, the absorption-in, the rapture ;
that which was meant to be and intended for a
verification, flowing from the fullness of life,
becomes instead detached from life ;  the soul
wants to deal only with God ; it is as if she desired
to exercise her love for him on him alone, and not
on his world.  Now, the soul thinks, the world
has disappeared ; it is no longer standing between
her and God.  But with the world God himself
has disappeared, and only she alone, the soul, is
left.  What she now calls God is only a figment in
herself, the dialogue which she thinks she is
carrying on is only a monologue with divided roles,
for the real partner in the communion is no longer
there.

Spinoza lived at a time when spiritual and
cultural independence again joined each other.
When the western world became aware of its
estrangement from God, it did not seek to turn its
worldly life towards God ; instead it tried to unite
itself with him by returning to him in mystical
and sacramental exaltation, leaving the world
outside.  The movement spilled over into art, and
there it crystallised itself as that fantastic flight of
fancy which we call the Baroque period.  From
the whole of Spinoza's mental and spiritual attitude
it is obvious that to him it was this pretence at a
communion which constituted the really impure.
Not outside the world, rather only in the world
itself, can man find the divine.  It is this thesis
which Spinoza sets in opposition to that dualism of
life which had become current in his time.  In

doing so Spinoza acts on an *ur*-Jewish instinct ; it is the very same instinct which once made the prophets protest against the independent, sacrificial cult.   But Spinoza's attack goes beyond its legitimate object ;   not only does the communion with God held apart from the world become unbelievable to him, but personal communion with God becomes also unbelievable.   His insight tells him that God cannot be spoken to apart from the world, because it is in the world itself that God is speaking ;   but he falsifies what he has thus seen by concluding that there is no speech between God and man.   From being the place of meeting with God, the world becomes, to him, God's place.

Although neither the speaker nor the hearer of the chassidic message knew anything about Spinoza, their message may still be taken as an answer to him ;   it is an answer to him, because it framed the creed of Israel anew, and in such a way that it did become an answer.   From of old Israel has proclaimed that the world is not God's place, but that God is ' the place of the world ', and that yet he lives within it.   Chassidism expresses this principle in a new way, namely, in a practical way. Because God is immanent in the world, the world becomes—in a general religious sense—a sacrament. If the world is God's place, it cannot be a sacrament ;   it is only the fact that the God who transcends the world is yet also immanent in it which can turn the world into a sacrament.   This, however, is not a purely objective statement, which remains true independently of the life lived by the individual ;   but still less is it a statement which is emprisoned in subjectivity ;   it is only when it is brought into actual contact with the individual that the world becomes sacramental.   That is, in the actual contact of these things and beings with this individual, with you, with me.   In all of these things and beings dwells the divine spark, and all

of these things and beings are given to this particular individual that this particular individual
may through his contact with them redeem the
divine spark.  Man's existence in the world becomes fraught with meaning, because the things
and beings of the world have been given to him in
their sacramental potentiality.  Spinoza's world
is a world which goes on existing beyond the life
which the individual man or woman has lived,
and beyond the death which the individual man or
woman is going to die, beyond my life and your
life ;  the chassidic world is the concrete world as
it is in this moment of a person's life ;  it is a world
ready to be a sacrament, ready to carry a real act of
redemption.  The world is that which is given us,
which is imposed upon us, which is offered us ;  it
is the medium in which God speaks to me and in
which he wills to receive his answer from me.
There is no room here for the self-sufficiency of
the soul who has mistaken her long-drawn-out self-
communion for the real dialogue in the All-Light.
God does not set himself apart from his creation.
But neither is there room for the metaphysical
construction which is erected by the soul who
fancies that she can see into Reality only when she
looks away from the lived situation, who imagines
that she is able to speak about God as if he sat like
a model for her conceptual constructions, as if he
were not hiding under the paraphernalia belonging
to the moment of reasoning, a secret which cannot
be presented in any definition, but which yet
appears, speaks, offers itself in and through the
concreteness of the given situation—and which is
pushed aside without an answer by all metaphysics.

By its fundamental principle of the actual
acceptance of God in things, the chassidic message
completes and widens the ancient teaching of
Israel.  It is a completion:  In all sections of the
Law do we find that ' Be ye holy, even as I am

holy ', not as a command for the gradual sanctification of mankind apart from things, but as a command that mankind as its contribution towards
creation shall step by step sanctify things. But
the chassidic message is also a widening: In
ancient Israel the sacrifice was the cultural sister of
the meal, which could not exist without it ; the
sacrifice was a sanctification of a part of the very
same organic matter of which the rest was given to
men for their nourishment. In the chassidic life
it is the eating itself which becomes a sacramental
service, it is the means whereby redemption comes
to the vegetable and animal nature ; through the
sanctifying acceptance of them as food the spark in
the animal and plant is set free. The distinction
made by the Law between clean and unclean
animals makes for an exclusion and a limitation,
but this is counter-acted by the extension of the
sanctifying power to all use of things ; the exclusion made on principle of a part of nature from
sanctification is on principle overcome. All that
has been allotted to man for his use, from cattle
and trees to fields and ploughs, hides a spark which
yearns to be lifted up through this man, and which
can be lifted up by the holy use this man makes of
what is given him ; even man's meeting with
strange things and strange creatures in a strange
land may carry the Holy Act. But more than that,
the separation has also been healed in the souls
of men. In the same way as the things and
creatures with which man has to deal are given to
him, so is also all that given him which comes to
his mind in imagination, in thought, in wish, and
stand before him in alien garb. In *all* is found
the mounting spark, pleading to be set free.
Nothing is unholy in itself, nothing is evil in itself ;
what we call evil is only the undirected storming
and collision of the unredeemed sparks in their
need for redemption. It is the passion—it is

even thus the very same energy which, when given direction, the ONE direction, brings forth the true good, the true service, redemption. The worldly and the spiritual lie no longer qualitatively separated side by side in the human soul; there is only the energy and the direction. He who divides his life between God and the world, giving the world what belongs to it in order to save for God what belongs to him, refuses to give God the service commanded by him, that service which consists in giving the one direction to all energy, the sanctification of the everyday in the world and in the soul.

The *ur*-evil of all ' religion ', the separation of ' living in God ' from ' living in the world ' is overcome in the chassidic message, and a true, concrete unity takes its place; moreover, the chassidic message gives also the answer to that false mastering of the distinction between God and man which consists in an abstract cancellation of it. The complete unity of the God who is both removed from and transcendent to the world, and who yet dwells within it, re-instates the undivided wholeness of human life in its full meaning; there is an acceptance of the world from God's hand, and an acting on the world to make it exist for God's sake. Accepting and acting, tied to the world, stands man, but not merely ' man ', rather is it this particular man, you, I, who stand thus in the immediate presence of God.

It was this teaching of man's union with the world in God's sight, this answer to Spinoza's teaching, given by Chassidism, which struck so deeply into my life. Already from boyhood I had dimly perceived, even while I defended myself against seeing it, that I was inevitably destined to love the world.

And the other question—but it is not another question, it is the very same question.

What is this we hear about the world's need for redemption ? But what is this we hear about God's indwelling in the world, this ' that he dwells in it in its defilement ' ? It is essentially the same question. The defilement of creation and its need for redemption are one and the same thing ; that God dwells in his creation and that God will redeem it are also one and the same thing.

The defilement of creation and not only of man ; the indwelling of God in the world and not only the indwelling of God in the soul ; it is from this we must start if we want to understand what the chassidic message says about redemption.

What we call evil is found not only in man, it is also the Evil in the world ; it is the defilement of creation. But this defilement is nothing positive, it is not an existing character of things. It is only their lack of firmness, their lack of direction, their vacillation.

God has created a world, and he has pronounced his creation to be very good—from whence then comes the evil ? God has created a world, and he rejoiced at its completion—from whence then comes the incomplete ?

The gnosis of all ages has posited another *ur*-power which stands over against the good power of God and works that which is evil ; gnosis wants to exhibit history as a fight between these two powers, and its victorious consummation as the redemption of the world. But we know what the nameless prophet proclaimed, he whose words are found in the second part of the *Book of Isaiah*: That as light and darkness were both created by God, so also are good and evil. Nothing uncreated stands over against him.

But in that case is not, after all, the bad and the evil a being, and an existing quality ? But even darkness is not a being, it is an abyss of lack of light and the struggle for light, and as such it was created by God.

The Bible presents evil as having penetrated into creation through an act of the first human beings. But it knows of somebody else who prompted this act, and therefore an evil, non-human creature, the serpent. The kabbalistic teaching, which Chassidism built into its own system, shifts the penetration of evil back into genesis. The Kabbalah teaches that the stream of fire of the creative grace poured itself out over ' the vessels ', the first *ur*-forms, in all its fullness ; but the vessels could not stand with it, they ' broke in pieces '—and the stream flashed forth into the infinity of ' sparks ', the ' shells ' grew round them, lack, defilement, evil came into the world. From now on does the incomplete cleave to the completed creation ; a suffering world, a world in need of redemption, lies at God's feet. But he does not leave it to lie alone in the abyss of its struggles ; his Glory itself descends to the world, following the sparks of his creative passion ; his Glory goes into it, goes into Exile, living in it ; his Glory lives with the sorrowful, suffering, created things in the midst of their defilement— eager to redeem them.

Although the Kabbalah does not openly admit it, it is yet unmistakably clear that its teaching firmly embraced the conception that already those *ur*-vessels, like the first human beings, had been allotted a movement of their own, an independence and a freedom, were it only the freedom to stand firm with the stream of grace or not to stand firm. The sin of the first human beings is thus presented as a not standing firm: Everything has been granted them, the whole fullness of grace is theirs, not even the tree of life is withheld from them ; only the knowledge of that which would

limit them, of the relation between the original
purity and the subsequent impurity of creation, only
the secret of the first being found lacking, the
secret of ' Good and Evil ' has God kept for himself.   But they cannot stand firm with the abundance of grace, they follow the promptings of the
element of limitation.   It is not that they raise
themselves against God, it is rather that they do
not rise up for him.   This 'stretching out of the
hand ' is not a rebellious movement, it is a helpless, undirected, irresolute, negligent gesture ;  they
do not do it, they have done it.   One can see in it
the undirected storming and rushing of the sparks
in need of redemption ;  temptation, turmoil, and
undecided act.   And so they ' know ' the limited,
even as men know, as Adam after this ' knew ' his
wife.   They know the limited, they intermingle
with it ;  they know ' Good-and-Evil ', they take
this ' Good-and-Evil ' up into themselves, as they
took into themselves the picked and eaten fruit.

It is then a not standing firm.   We know of it,
we to whom the situation in which the first human
beings found themselves returns day after day,
always again for the first time, always repeated ;
we know of this suffering act, which is nothing but a
reaching out from the undirected whirl ;  we know
of the sparks, how they storm and tumble about
and get entangled in themselves ;  we know that
what moves our badness is really our need for
redemption, our search for redemption.   And perhaps we also know the emergence of the Other
from those hidden, unimaginable moments, the
softest unfolding, the receiving of direction, the
deciding, the turning of the swirling movement of
the world towards God.   Here we have an immediate experience of the fact that self-movement,
independence, freedom are given to us.   Whatever
may be the case with the non-human part of
creation, we know from the character which the

Creator has given to men that he sent man into
the world with power to do two things, and to do
them in reality, and not only to imagine for a brief
moment of self-deception that he could do them.
Man can choose God, or he can reject God ; that
man may fall implies that he may rise ; that man has
power to lead the world to destruction implies
that he has power to lead the world to redemption.

However literally many a religion and many a
theology may take these two powers of man to be,
even when they envisage them only as the mere
capacity to believe or to withhold belief, they still
constitute the actual admission of man into that
which is All-mighty. And it is this which remains
the core of all religious life, just as it is the very core
of all human life. However literal this admission
is taken to be, the fact remains that the creation of
this being, man, means that God has made room
for a co-determining power, for a starting-point
for events, for a beginning. Not once in his life
was man free to choose or to reject God, or rather,
to leave him unchosen, man is always free. Does
this mean that God has given away one iota of his
power to determine the course of events ? We only
ask that question, when we are busy subsuming
God under our logical categories. In our moments
of vision we have an immediate experience of our
freedom, and yet in these moments we also know
by an immediate experience that God's hand has
carried us. It is these moments which show us
how, from out of our own personal life, we can draw
hear to the secret in which man's freedom and
God's determining power, man's reality and God's
reality, are no longer contradictory.

But one may also ask another question: The
first human beings were free before they fell away
from God ; and does that mean that God had not
willed what they did ? And how can anything
happen without God willing it ? No theological

argumentation can help us here, only the firmly held realisation that God's thoughts are not like our thoughts, that his will not like our will is held firmly fast and then rubbed away by time and tide and subsequent events. We may say that God wills that man should choose him and not fall away from him; but we have to add to that, God also wills that his world shall be a way; and more than that: In order that this may be so in reality, he wills that his creatures shall go the way themselves, they must go in their own persons, from out of their own personality, and always and again in their own personality; the fall must be as real as the redemption; and the man, the creature, as he has the power really to fall so has he the power really to effect the work of redemption from out of his own self, man, in whom the course of the world is reflected. Does that mean that God cannot redeem the world without man's help? It means that God would not even do that. Has God need of man for his work? He wills to have need of man.

God wills to use man for the completion of his work of creation. This sentence gives the foundation of the Jewish doctrine of redemption. But it is God's will so to use man, and that means that the use of man for this work becomes an effective reality. In history as it actually unfolds itself before our eyes we see that God waits for man.

It is not appearance that God has gone into exile by his indwelling in the world; it is not appearance that he suffers by his immanence the fate of the world. And it is not appearance that he waits in order that the initial movement towards redemption should come from the world itself— an initiating by the world not in appearance only. How it happens that this is not appearance but reality, how it happens that something from out of his own world, be it a falling away or a returning to him, can come upon God, the All-mighty and

All-knowing, that is the mystery which belongs to God, the Creator and Redeemer, not more mysterious to me than that he is ; and that he is, is far less mysterious to me than that I am, the I who am writing this with trembling hand, sitting on a rock above a lake.

It would be completely senseless to try to measure how great is man's part in the redemption of the world.   There is not any part that belongs to man, or any part that belongs to God ; there is no as far as here, and there is no from there ; there is nothing that can be measured and weighed here. It is even false to speak of any collaboration.   This applies to all human life and perhaps to all life of the created world ; it is senseless to ask how far my action reaches, and  where God's grace begins ; there is no common border-line ; what concerns me alone, before I bring something about, is my action, and what concerns  me alone, when the action is successfully done, is God's grace.   The one is no less real than the other, and neither is a part-cause.   God and man do not divide the government of the world between them ; man's action is enclosed in God's action, but it is still real  action.

Thus each moment of a person's life is really set between creation and redemption ; it falls within creation in that it is made, it is tied and bound to redemption in virtue of its power for making ; or rather, it is not so much set between the two as in both jointly.   Just as creation did not take place once and for all at the beginning of time, but happens all the time throughout the whole of time, so redemption will not come to pass at the end of time, but happens all the time throughout the whole of time.   Each moment of a person's life is not just placed within creation and within redemption, rather are creation and redemption contained in it.   Creation did not ' really ' happen once and for all and somehow is merely being continued at this very moment so that all creative acts from the very first to the one which is being done at this very moment add up to the sum total of creation ; on the contrary, the true point of view is given in the prayer that God will renew his creative work every day ; the act of creation which still happens has complete power to begin something new, and the moment in which God's creative act happens is not set in a time-series only, but has also its own unconditioned existence. As in the sphere of creation in which God alone acts the moment does not just come from somewhere, but comes in its own right and in itself, so it is also in the sphere of redemption, where God permits, yea demands, that his work shall be enclosed in the work of man, however incomprehensible the mode of this may be to us. The moment of redemption is real not only with respect to its fulfilment, but also in itself ; the moments of redemption cannot be added up ; although they form a series, yet each of them reaches the secret of fulfilment ; each of them is the bearer not only of a goal, but also of a meaning ; each of them takes its place in the time-series on the moving canvas of the world's history, and there counts in its place ; but each of them also bears its own testimony, sealed up within it, and distinct from that of all the others. This, however, does not mean that each moment becomes a mysterious, timeless now ; rather does it mean that each moment is filled with all time: In the hovering fraction of time, the fulness of time is manifested. From the meeting of God and man there issues no mere events in the life of the soul, but from out of this meeting vital events come upon the world. It is ' the downflowing of the blessing '.

The knowledge of the redemption of the every-day came to Chassidism both by esoteric and exoteric tradition; the chassidic message has proclaimed the knowledge in its practical form. Chassidism turned against the whole monstrous system of kabbalistic instructions, against the powerful efforts of ' he who hurries the End '; there does not exist a certain, demonstrable, trans-mittable, teachable, magic-making acting with established formulae and gestures, with spiritual attitudes and tensions, which will have an effect on the redemption of the world; only the indis-criminate consecration of all acts, only the turning of the normal life towards God as it happens from day to day, only the hallowing of the natural union with the world, have the redeeming power. The everyday of redemption grows only out of the redemption of every day.

The chassidic answer to that catastrophe of the Jewish messianism which goes by the name of Sabbatai Zwi is based on the above teaching. This is so not only within the truth of history, but also within actual reality.

It is a mistake to regard the Jewish teaching about the Messiah merely as a belief in a unique, final event and in a unique, human being as the centre of this event. The sureness of the exist-ence of the co-operating power which is allotted to man, even to the human race, links the end of the world with the present life. Already in the prophetic writings of the first Exile we find mysteri-ous references to the succession of ' the servants of God ' who, arising in generation after genera-tion, will carry and purify the defilement of the world, contemned and held in low esteem by their fellow-men. Later writings add references to an esoteric view of world-history, according to which also the great persons in the biblical narratives have a messianic character. Each of them was called, each of them denied his calling in some respect, the diverse sins of each implied his denial

of the messianic calling. So God waits throughout the generations of men for the one in whom the
absolutely essential, necessary movement arising
from the creature will win for him the decisive
power. With the deepening of the exile of the
world, which has occurred through the exile of
Israel, the men who arise in each generation are
no longer known to the world, but live in seclusion ;
they do their work no longer in the light of accessible history, but in the darkness belonging to an
inaccessible, personal work of suffering, of which
no account, not even inaccurate accounts, reach the
outside world. But the more the fate of the world
becomes filled with suffering, the fate of that
world with which God suffers through his immanence in it, the more do the lives of these men become filled with meaning and operative in themselves. They are no longer as it were foreshadowings of the messianic form, rather in them
is the messiahship belonging to the end of time
preceded by one of all time, poured out over the
ages ; without this the fallen world could not
continue in existence. It is true that these men
are only attempts made by the creature, they are
forerunners, but yet the messianic power itself is
in them. ' The Messiah, the son of Joseph, appears
from generation to generation '. This is the
suffering Messiah, who always, again and again,
for God's sake, suffers mortal pain.

This messianic *mysterium* stands or falls with
its seclusion ; not because it is kept secret, but
because it is in itself a true, actual seclusion which
penetrates to the innermost existence. The men to
whom it comes are those whom the nameless
prophet spoke of in his own name, when he said
that God had made him a polished shaft, and then
hidden him in his quiver. Their hiddenness belongs essentially to their work of suffering. Each
of them can be the Promised One ; none of them

dare in their own self-consciousness be anything but a servant of God. With the tearing apart of their seclusion not only would their work itself be destroyed, but a counter-work would supervene upon it. Messianic self-disclosure is the disruption of the messiahship.

In order rightly to understand the attitude of Jewry to the appearance of Jesus one must descend to the depth of the faith which is not included in any confessions, but which can be shown from its manifestations. Whatever meaning the appearance of Jesus carried for the Gentiles (and its meaning for the Gentiles remains, to me, the real seriousness in western history), as seen from the point of view of Jewry, Jesus is the first in the series of men who acknowledged to themselves in their souls and openly in their words their messiahship, and thus they stepped out of the seclusion of the servants of God, which is the real ' messianic secret '. That this First One—as I always again experience, when the strong, personal words that ring so true come together into a unity for me, so that their speaker becomes real to me— that this First One was the incomparably purest, most righteous of them all, the one most endowed with messianic power, does not alter the fact that he was the first, yea, it belongs rather to it, it belongs to that awful, penetrating character of reality which clings to the whole messianic series.

It is also due to this characteristic of the series, I suppose, that the last of them all—that one, Sabbatai Zwi, who died in the same year as Spinoza— falls a victim to the deepest of the problems, and slides over from the true self-knowledge to a pretended one, and ends in secession. And, unlike his predecessors, just this one was not followed by a small band of adherents, but the whole of Jewry fell for his teaching, and accepted from him as a true message words which in olden times used to be anathema to them, and which they used to consider to be evidence against the truth of the calling. It was a Jewry disordered in the abyss of suffering, it is true, but it was yet the bearer of a real crisis, the self-destruction of the auto-messiahship. Until Sabbatai Zwi appeared, the people had held out against the proclamations of the ' meshichim ' and against its own thirst for redemption. Now when it for once gave up resistance, the catastrophe put an end not only to the one appearance whom the people had followed, but also to the whole form of the appearance, that is to the meeting of the man who takes the far-reaching decision to swing over from being the hidden servant of God to the acknowledgement of his consciousness of his own messiahship with a band who takes it upon itself to begin the Kingdom of God on earth.

In our time we would take it as self-evident that we were here confronted with the confluence of two self-delusions, the one a personal one, the other belonging to the herd-instinct. But if we are to understand what I have tried so far to describe, we must realise that we are not dealing with self-delusions only, we are dealing with the real trespassing of a real boundary. It is a trespassing so great that the fearful responsibility of it makes the man who undertakes it respond as sensitively and as tremblingly as the magnetic needle. The events of the auto-messianic epoch in the Jewish teaching of redemption (to which corresponds on the Christian side baptism in its various forms) constitute a series of errors, but they were errors in the realm of the reality of God and man.

After the catastrophe, after the decisive inner fall of Sabbatai Zwi from self-truth to self-lie, which preceded the outer fall, there is no longer any real auto-messianism in the sense of a real meeting between one human being and a band of followers ; it degenerated into literature, as for instance with the genius Moses Chajim Luzzatto,

or into swindle, as with Jakob Frank, who yet once
again bewitched Polish Jewry into a short dream ;
and then he seceded to Christianity, as Sabbatai
Zwi had seceded to Islam.

That was already at the time of Baalshem. A
tradition, which is questioned by historians, lets
Baalshem take part in a disputation of the Polish
rabbis against Frank a year before his death. But
far greater, and unquestionable in its essential
truth, is the struggle in the loneliest stillness of the
heart of which legend speaks. Here, as elsewhere,
legend gathers into one event a whole attitude to
life. In the legend we see Baalshem rise again and
again against the degenerate auto-messianism, teaching, influencing, destroying the illusion, prevent-
ing false actions from happening, and also working
directly against the auto-messianism. But perhaps we find the strongest testimony of it in the
story of his temptation.

It may be taken for granted that in the life of
every person who is a founder, there occurs one
central story of a temptation, even though all has
not been told. It is characteristic for the kind and
call of the individual how, and by whom, and
through what, he is tempted. For Baalshem it is
the dead Sabbatai Zwi who is the tempter. First
he asks Baalshem to save him. But a salvation of
this kind can only happen if one binds one's own
being to that of the dead, soul to soul, spirit to
spirit. Baalshem began to do this, but only care-
fully and little by little, lest the evil should injure
himself. When during the work of salvation
Sabbatai Zwi once again appeared to Baalshem in a
dream, he tempted him, but Baalshem pushed him
away, and he fell down again to the abyss. ' A
holy spark ', said the Master himself later about
Sabbatai Zwi, ' lived in him, but Sammael has
caught him in the coils of pride '.

It is obvious that we are meant to understand
the temptation of auto-messianism by the tempta-

tion which the legend gives us. The stand made against the suggestion of being the Messiah introduces a new precedence.

It is true that after the death of Baalshem his pupils hinted that his soul would return in the Messiah. It is true that in later Chassidism even ' he who hurried the End ' came to life again. But the message remains.

The chassidic message of redemption should be understood in connection with the attitude which Baalshem took to redemption. It rises against the messianic self-differentiation between one man and the other men, between one age and the other ages, between one act and the other acts. To the whole of mankind is given the power to co-operate, all ages stand immediately face to face with the power to redeem, all action for God's sake may be called messianic action. But only simple-hearted action can be action for God's sake. The self-differentiation, the anaclasis of men by a messianic privilege belonging to this or that man, to this or that hour, to this or that action, destroys the unpremeditated quality of the act. To turn the whole of the life of the world towards God and then to let it spread and to relinquish it in all moments even till the last, that is men's work towards redemption.

We live in an unredeemed world. But from each tied, worldly-bound life of man falls a seed of redemption. And the harvest is God's.

# Symbolism and Sacramental Existence in Judaism

## 1 : *The symbolic existence in the world of prophecy*

Human existence is in its relation to symbols and sacraments not only the place in which they appear, and not only the material in which they clothe themselves. The factual existence of a human being can itself be a symbol, a sacrament.

It does not belong to the nature of symbols to hover timelessly over concrete actualities. Whenever the symbol appears, it owes its appearance always to the unsuspected, unique occasion, to its having appeared the first time. The symbol draws its endurance from a transitory event. It is true that when we stand on the brink of the lived world, we acknowledge that all which is transitory is ' only ' a likeness ; but when we live in the world, we learn that only that which is transitory can become a likeness. For the image of the unrefracted meaning, for its proper expression, compared with which all that we call language is only estimation, serves always in the first instance nothing but our born, mortal body—everything else is only repetition, simplification, imitation. The spiritual together with its timelss working forms a compact whole, it does not point to something beyond itself ; the body, time's prisoner, it alone can be made transparent in its fleeting gestures. The covenant which the Absolute enters into with the concrete, far beyond the general, the ' idea ', chooses always for itself a sign which is more fleeting than the rainbow of Noah's covenant ; it chooses movements made by the human figure, be it movements of posture or of action. And this sign endures. It may lose in immediate validity, in ' evidential value ', but it may also renew itself from later human existence, which anew fulfils itself. All symbols are ever in danger of becoming spiritual, and unconnected, images, instead of remaining real signs sent into life; all sacraments are ever in danger of becoming superficial, personal, experiences, levelled down to the ' religious ' plane, instead of remaining the incarnate connection between what is above and what is below. Only through the man who lets himself go is the original power saved for further present existence.

Plato distinguishes in the *Timaeus* (72B) be-

tween the ' mantis ', the diviners, whom he takes
to be ' manentes ', raving, distraught by God, and
who receive from the gods in mysterious sounds
that which they 'divine', and the 'prophetai', the
' interpreters ', who interpret the secret hid in
the sound, and translate it into human speech.
When Pindar* assigns the part of ' divination ' to
the muse, and the part of ' interpreting ' to the
poet, then nothing more has happened than that
the passive element of the former has been pressed
into the background : the essential relationship
remains the same ; the muse gives the poet her
primitive theme, he embodies it in words and verse ;
but the muse does not utter what is hers, but what
belongs to the God, to her Lord Apollon, by whom
she, a superhuman pythia, is possessed. But, as
Apollon himself acknowledges in Aeschylos,† even
he also serves as mantis and prophet combined a
higher power, Zeus, who endows him with knowledge ; Apollon gives it out, but the one who
seizes what he says, be it muse or pythia, holds no
words, but only the secret, which he lisps forth but
cannot say, until at last he who hears it, the
' prophetic ' interpreter, proclaims it.

The ' manteia ', the divination, is not yet for
the Greeks a ' finished ' speech. It breaks forth,
untrammelled, not to be comprehended by the
unprophetic man ; only by the prophet is it first
comprehended and formed into logos. The prophet
translates, but from a language which is no language
to the ear of him who is not called. We must take
it that when a man unites both functions, he acts
first as mantis and then as prophet ; instead of a
differentiation in persons comes a differentiation
in matter, a change in the person. The duality
remains.

Not so with the biblical nawi. It is in the first

---

* *Fragment*, 150.
† *Eumenides*, vv. 17 ff. (cp. 615 ff.)

instance not without significance that here the conception is not used also in a secular sense, as it is
in Greek, where one might also call the exponent
of a philosophy, or. even the announcer in an
athletic game, a prophet, using the word in the
sense of a man who proclaims or announces something.  The nawi exists only in the relation of
deity and humanity, as the mediator of the language,
' the bearer of the word in the vertical plane ',*
and not only from above to below as the bringer of
a divine message, but also from below to above :
It is as ' herald ' that Abraham shall ' take his
place as mediator ' for the King of Philistia (this
is the original meaning of the Hebrew term for
' to pray ') ; it is as ' herald ' that Miriam sings,
as ' herald ' that Deborah sings their triumph
songs of thanksgiving.  It is the nawi's duty to
let the speech spoken between deity and humanity
fulfil itself.  The God chooses for himself this
messenger from his ' mother's womb ', so that,
through him, the original call of admonition or
promise may reach the ear of him who is to receive
it, but also that the cry from the heart of the
creature may gather itself in him and be lifted up.
It is true that the divine intention does not aim at
mediacy but at immediacy ; but the mediator is
the way to the immediacy, to the desired time when
all God's people shall be heralds and bearers of the
spirit (*Numbers*, 11.29).

The biblical nawi-conception is seen most
clearly in a passage (*Exodus*, 7.1) in which it is used
as a simile of the relationship between two people
who are to each other exactly what the elohim, the
power of God, and the nawi, its herald, are to each
other :  ' See, ' says God to Moses, ' I give you to
Pharoah for an elohim,/ and Aaron, your brother,
shall be your nawi '.  The simile lets here both of

---

* Buber, *Konigtum Gottes* (1932), p. 165.

them, elohim, the incoming power, and nawi, the expressing being, appear unmistakably in their mutual relationship. How intimate this mutual relationship is conceived to be is shown at an earlier stage of the story by a parallel passage (*Exodus*, 4.16) : ' He shall then speak for you to the people,/ and it shall be thus :/ he shall be to you a mouth, and you shall be to him an elohim '. To be the nawi of an elohim means then to be his ' mouth '. His mouth, not his megaphone. The nawi does not convey a finished speech, which has already been made articulate, he terminates a hidden, soundless speech, the speech which in the human mind is pre-verbal, and in the divine mind *ur*-verbal, as the mouth of a person terminates the secret, soundless speech of his innermost being. This fundamental conception reaches its full pathos, when God speaks of his relationship to the nawi and uses just this image, and the biblical distance between God and man is only still kept by God not saying ' my mouth ', but ' as my mouth '. Jeremiah has in a critical moment besought God for revenge over his persecutors (*Jeremiah*, 15.15). He who answers him does not merely ignore the matter in which the prophet has been untrue to his office, he indicates to him (vv. 19ff.) that only when he finds himself back again on God's way from the all too human way on which he has gone and lost himself, will he re-instate him and let him stand ' before his face ', ' And if you bring forth what is true,/ emptied of what is base,/ you shall be as my mouth '.

It is of decisive importance to notice that God does not here pronounce that he will use the human mouth as his own, *the whole human being* shall be to him as a mouth.

The Greek prophet is not this, he cannot be this. His mouth ' speaks forth ', not his person. But also the mantis is not this, and cannot be this.

His person, seized upon and possessed by God,
utters words, but it itself pronounces nothing. So
long as a person functions as mantis he is unin-
telligible to him who receives the utterance ; as
soon as he becomes his own prophet, he is only the
speaker of a word with which he himself has
nothing to do.

In the biblical world of faith there are not two
persons who stand beside God, one immediately,
the other mediately ; there is only one person,
even he whom the divine ' storm of the spirit '
blows into ' to clothe itself with him ' (*Judges*,
6.34), even he it is who is not only with his linguistic
tools, but rather with his whole being and life,
speaker for the hidden voice which blows through
him, that ' silence soaring aloft ' (1 *Kings*, 19.12).

' Pythia and interpreting priestly poet were not
here divided ; the Israelitic prophet was both in
one ', writes Max Weber. For the prophetic
word in the Bible, as distinct from the word of the
Delphic Oracle, this means that the rising speech
and the finished speech are biblically identical,
whereas the Hellenic speech is an ecstatic babbling
which first must be translated before it can become
proper speech. The speech which breaks forth
from the biblical herald is the speech which is cast
into words, it is rhythmically formed, ' objective '
speech. And yet it is not words which can be
separated from the herald, words which are only
' laid in his mouth ' ; his whole personal being as
a speaker belongs to his speech, the whole speaking,
human body, the ensouled body which is now
inspired by the ruach, the pneuma, the whole
existence of this human being belongs to the
speech, the whole human being is a mouth.

Here there is no division between a passion of
the ' manesthai ', of possession and trance, and an
action of ' proeipein ', of the mastering, forming
speech. The form of the speech is not here ' put

on ', it is born in the initial urge for articulation—
wherefore also for example all metrical scansion
must necessarily always fail in the hand of the
scholar, as the ' ready-made ' metre is every time
overthrown by the once-occurring stream of prophecy. The person who is seized by the ruach and
pressed to words does not stammer before he
speaks ; he still speaks ' in the grasp of the hand ',
a strictly rhythmical speech, but one through which
yet the cascading fullness of the moment rushes.

Also the thesis of ' a development ' from
' primitive ecstatic ' to ' word prophet ' leads one
astray ; in the Bible the ecstatic never appears
except in conjunction with the word prophet ; it
is true that we read about wild and ' raving ', but
not unmusical, behaviour, but we do not read of
babbling or of unarticulated shouting, we come to
know the voice of the nawi only as word, and his
word only as speech. Passion and action are here
also in historical time not divided but one. We are
here dealing with one single, inclusive function,
and the undivided person is necessary to establish
the indivisible function.

But in order rightly to grasp the nature of
prophetic existence, it is necessary also to consider
the purpose of prophecy.

Both, the Greek word of the oracle as well as
the biblical word of the nawi, are tied to the
situations in which they arise. But the oracle
gives answers to a situation which is brought before
it as a question by emissaries who ask for information ; the nawi, sent by God, speaks unasked into
the biographical or historical situation. The
answer of the oracle is prediction of an unalterable
future, the warning of the nawi implies the indeterminism and determining power of the hour. In
the first case the future is written down on a scroll,
and the unfolding of the scroll constitutes what
happens in history ; in the second case nothing

has been set down ; over the freely oscillating
replies of man to the approaching events God holds
mysteriously his shadowing hands ; his power,
which is greater and more mysterious than the
statutory ' omnipotence ' of dogma, is able to
reserve some powerfulness for the moment of the
creature.

In Herodotus (I.91) the pythia declares that
it is also impossible for a God to elude the destined
fate. The paradigmatic *Book of Jonah* tells how
God through a nawi has let it be proclaimed to the
sinful city of Nineveh that it is to be destroyed,
not a conditional destruction which can be averted,
' Yet forty days, and Nineveh shall be overthrown '
sounds the call of the prophet.* Nineveh, however,
has completed the turning of its repentance, and
now the God is also ' turned '. This reciprocal
relationship of turning had been the secret meaning
of the message, unknown to the prophet himself,
and afterwards unwelcome to him. It is therefore
a legitimate exposition of biblical faith, when
Jewish tradition says of the prophets that they have
' only prophesied to those who turn '.† The nawi
advises the people of a situation with reference to
the actual, determining power which these people
possess. His speech is not merely relative to a
situation. Its tie with the situation reaches to the
secret ground in which existence is rooted in
creation. And just because his speech conceives
the moment in this way and corresponds to it in
this way does it remain valid for all generations and
all nations.

Prophecy takes its stand on the reality of history
as it is happening. Against all mantic historio-
sophia, all officious knowledge of the future,
whether of a dialectic or of a gnostic origin, it sets
the insight into the true nature of that which is

---

* 3. 4.
† *Babyl-Talmud*, tr. Berachot, 34*b*.

happening, into the moment which is determined by so many things, and which yet in the single-heartedness of its decisions is truly determining itself.

The spoken word alone cannot, however, satisfy the determining power of the moment. In order to be equal to it, in order to meet it in its boundless reality, the spoken word needs to be supplemented by the power of the attitude and actions of significant signs. Only together with this is it possible for the spoken word to present and to invoke the power of determination. Not the word by itself has effect on reality, only the word set into the whole existence of a human being, appearing from the whole of his existence, associated with the whole of him.

Biblically, a sign can include a proof or a confirmation ; according to its nature it is neither. One example of many may show this. To Moses' objection, ' Who am I, that I should go to Pharoah,/ that I should lead the sons of Israel out of Egypt ! ' God answers, ' Certainly, I will be with you,/ and this is the sign for you that I myself send you : / when you have led the people out of Egypt,/ then shall you serve God on this mountain ' (*Exodus*, 3.12). This ' sign ' is not to be taken as a confirmation. But biblically a sign means something else : Incarnation. The biblical person, and with him the biblical God, demands that the spirit shall speak in a more perfect, more exact, way than the word, that it shall incarnate itself. When man demands this utterance of God, it is called in biblical language, to demand a sign, that is, to demand corporeality of the message. When God demands this utterance of man, it is called, to ' tempt ' a person, that is, to draw out of a person what hides itself in him, to bring him to account ; thus God tempts Abraham (*Genesis*, ch. 22) in that he, terrible in his mercifulness, grants him the extreme possibility of showing him his innermost devotion. But God wills also that man should desire of him the incarnation of the spirit ; he who demands a sign of him is borne out in his demand ; the man who will not receive the sign which God offers him shows not faith, but lack of faith (*Isaiah*, 7.11–13). The mission given to Moses from the burning bush incarnates itself in ' signs ', as the people who have been led out of the service in Egypt has come to the burning mountain and now will serve the God who has brought them unto himself ' on eagles' wings ' (*Exodus*, 19.4).

The sign cannot be translated, ' word ' cannot be substituted for it, one cannot look up in any book of signs what a sign means ; but the spoken word completes itself in the sign, and becomes corporeal. The spoken word itself belongs to it, but only in its being spoken, as a sort of corporeal attitude and act.

Only what is transitory can be a likeness. Both of them, sign and likeness, are not soluble ; no pronouncement can be made out of both ; both express what cannot be expressed in any other way ; body and image cannot be paraphrased ; body, like image, gives first the depth of the word ; and corporeal signs are no proof, as the likeness in images is no comparison.

The prophesying of the nawi, which is no soothsaying business, but its exact contrary, con-templates an event whose occurrence or non-occurrence depends on the either-or of the moment. Such a contemplated event, however, can only be adequately expressed through a happening given in a sign. The fullness of determinations and the determining power which belong to the moment as the fountain-head of events can only be rightly given by a happening in signs, by a ' symbolic act '.

It is on the background of this that we can

understand all those acts which the biblical prophets did as signs, from the most fleeting ones, as when Jeremiah breaks in pieces a potter's earthen mug before the Elders, or when Ezekiel joins together two sticks of wood, to those which reach as far into life as Hosea marrying a whore and giving the children of this marriage names of deprecation. From an example like the last one, which surely is unsurpassed in its harshness, it becomes immediately clear that we are not dealing with life-like metaphors, but with a physical presentation in the strictest sense of the term. What here has to be shown in the world of men is the marriage between God and the whore Israel. ' Go', says the voice in its first declaration to the nawi, ' Go and take to yourself a whore as wife and children of whoredom,/*because* the country, practising prostitution, whores/away from ITS succession'. Unsurpassably harsh comes this ' because ' as God claims the lived life of his own called herald to be a sign, to be a material presentation of an experience of God's, his experience with Israel. What happens here is a holy act of terrible earnestness, it is a real sacramental drama. The account of the marriage and the immediate identification with God's words interlock with each other, moving us to terror in their harshness. The account has just been given of the naming of ' the children of the whoredom ', *i.e.*, the lawful children of Hosea and the whore. ' You-will-not-find-mercy' is one daughter called (' *because* I will not any more have mercy, have mercy/ on the house of Israel,/ that I should again be deceived by them, deceived '), ' Not-my-people ' is a son called (' *because* you are not my people/and I am not there for you ')— and then, suddenly (2.4) the voice of God speaks in the children to the children of Israel, ' Fight against your mother, fight !/For she is not my wife/ and I am not her husband !/She must take off her

whore's paint/from her face,/the adulteress's marks
from between her breasts ! ' We are here made to
see most keenly to what depths of reality the existence of ' the signs ' can reach.

The nawî does not merely act out a sign, he
lives it. Not what he does is in the last resort the
sign, but in that he does it he himself is the sign.

But it is in Isaiah (8.11–22) that the symbolic
existence of the prophet reaches both its highest
intensity and clarity. It is a time of the greatest
confusion in which the coming catastrophe of the
people announces itself ; truth and falsehood are
so intermingled that the soul is scarcely able to
distinguish, scarcely able to recognise what is right ;
God himself is being mistaken, misunderstood,
misused, ' for a snare and a trap by the settler in
Jerusalem '. It is true that there is also a comfort-
ing prophecy for this situation, which points beyond the coming catastrophe (it is found in our
*Book of Isaiah*, 9.1–6). But to formulate that now
would mean to give it over to being mistaken, misunderstood, misused. Therefore Isaiah says as the
word for the hour, ' It is necessary to tie up the
evidence,/to seal up the instruction/in my apprentices '. As one ties up and seals a document,
so does he with the prophecy which he administers
to his disciples: They themselves represent now
the sealed document, whose seal shall only be
broken, when, in the middle of the catastrophe, the
cry goes up to the people which in vain has run to
its ' chirping, muttering ' ' elves ' for oracle (v.19),
' To the evidence, to the confirmation ! ' Until
the time when God, who now ' hides his face from
the house of Jacob ' (v.17) will have mercy on ' the
remnant ' that turns to him, will the prophet
' tarry ' in the coming ' nightly dark fear' (v. 22) in
the midst of the people who ' have no shimmer of
dawn ', he and his ' apprentices ' and his own
children, of which he has given one the name of the

prophecy, ' the remnant-turns', obviously at God's command. And he expresses this ' tarrying ' in the following way (v.18), ' Very well,/I and the children, which HE has given me,/are there in Israel for a sign and a confirmation,/from HIM, the surrounded one,/ he who dwells on Mount Zion '. These people, the core of that ' holy remnant ' are there as signs, they live their independent lives, at the same time also as signs. It is this man who is with the whole of his being a sign, who is ' God's mouth '. Through his symbolic existence is said what there is to be said. And this is something different from much which we call a symbol. But no symbol, in no timeless height, can in any other way become and become again reality than by incarnating itself in such a living and dying human existence.

## 2: *The sacramental existence in the world of Chassidism*

A symbol is a manifestation of meaning, the appearance and becoming apparent of meaning in the form of corporeality. The covenant of the Absolute with the concrete is demonstrated in the symbol. But a sacrament is the act in which meaning is tied to body, it is the execution of the deed of covenant, it is to be tied, fastened, joined. The covenant of the Absolute with the concrete takes place in the sacrament.

A manifestation, taken as an event, has one direction, it goes from ' above ' to ' below ', that which appears enters into the corporeality which bears it. A covenant has two directions; what is above binds itself to that which is below, and what is below binds itself to that which is above ; what is above binds what is below, and what is below binds what is above ; they bind themselves to each other ; meaning and life bind each other.

Where a covenant is demonstrated it is like seeing the reflected image of a person, who himself is out of sight ; where the covenant takes place, it is like walking hand in hand. Hand in hand is the covenant made, and hand in hand is it renewed.

The foremost meaning of a sacrament, although not the only meaning, is that the divine and the human join themselves to each other, without merging themselves in each other, a lived life beyond transcendence and immanence. But also when it is only two human beings who consecrate themselves to each other sacramentally—in marriage. in brotherhood—is that other covenant, the covenant between the Absolute and the concrete consummated secretly ; for the consecration does not come by the power of the human partners, but by the power of the eternal wings that overshadow both. Everything unconditioned into which human beings enter with each other has its strength from the presence of that which is unconditioned.

The sacrament has rightly been called ' the most dynamic of all ritual forms '.* But what is of greatest importance about this its dynamic character is that it is stripped of its character, when it no longer includes a supreme, life-claiming, and life-determining experience of the other person, of the otherness, as a coming to meet and as an acting herewards. The three-dimensionality of the event, the existence of its depth of dimension, is given by the fact that the human being in the sacramental consecration neither merely ' commits ' something, nor, even less, merely ' experiences' something, that he is laid hold of and demanded in the core of his wholeness, and needs nothing less than his wholeness if he is to sustain it. The ecclesiastical convention, or other similar sacral conventions, levels the event

---

* R. R. Marett, *Sacraments of Simple Folk* (Oxford, 1933), p. 9.

down to gesture, while mystical religiosity presses it together to an ecstatically felt instant.

All sacraments have a natural mode of operation, taken from the natural course of life and consecrated in the sacrament, and a material or corporeal otherness, with which one comes in holy contact—in a contact in which the secret strength of the sacrament becomes effective in its work on one.

' Primitive ' man is a naive pansacramentalist. Everything is to him full of sacramental substance, everything, each thing and each function is ever ready to light up into a sacrament for him. He knows of no selection of objects and agencies, he knows only of methods and favourable times. ' It ' is everywhere, one has only to be able to catch it. There are formulae and rhythms for doing so, that is true, but one only acquires these too, when one ventures on it, and he who already is capable of knowing must always expose himself again and again to the dangerously appropriating and demanding contact.

The crisis of all primitive mankind comes with the discovery of that which is fundamentally not-holy, the a-sacramental, which withstands the method, and which has no ' hour ', a province which steadily enlarges itself. In some tribal communities, which we usually still call primitive, we can, even if only in some extreme individuals, observe this critical phase, in which the world threatens to become neutralised, and to deny itself to the holy contact. This is surely for example what the Ba-ila of Northern Rhodesia mean, when they say about their God, ' Leza has become old ', or ' Leza is not to-day any longer what he should be '.* What we call religion in a narrower sense has perhaps from time to time arisen in such a

---

* E. W. Smith and A. M. Dale, *The Ila-Speaking Peoples of Northern Rhodesia*, ii. 200 ff.

crisis. All historical religion is *selection* of sacramental material and sacramental acts. By separating the holy from the abandoned profane the sacrament is saved. The consecration of the covenant becomes concentrated in an objective-functional way.

But with this the sacrament enters into a new and more difficult problem. For a concrete religion can only then prove the reality of the seriousness with which it takes its demands, when it exacts of the faithful who have ' faith ' that they stake nothing less than the whole of their person. But the sacrament, which is founded on a division of the holy and the profane in its concentrated power, misleads the faithful into feeling secure in a merely ' 'objective ' consummation without any personal participation, in *opus operatum*, and to evade that they themselves in the whole of their being are laid hold of and claimed by the sacrament. To the extent, however, that the substance of the lives of the faithful ceases to graft itself into the sacrament does this lose in depth, in three-dimensional reality, in corporeality. It was this which happened for instance in biblical Israel : In the sacramental offer the faithful only let themselves be represented by the animal, the central intention remained that of bringing themselves, and it was this which withered away in the security of an objectively executed, ritual atonement.* Or, in the Bible the anointing of a king was the act by which a person was placed in a position of lifelong responsibility to God for the continued task entrusted to him of being God's vice-gerent ;† in the western rites of coronation this degenerated into a grandiose affirmation of personal power.

An attempt to re-establish, a reformation, may

---

* Cp. Buber, *Konigkum Gottes*, pp. 99 ff.
† Cp. my forthcoming book, *Der Gesalbte* (*Das Kommende, Untersuchungen zur Entstehungsgeschichte des menslichen Glaubens*, II Band.

succeed where the inner crisis of a given sacramentalism draws in question the original content of a religion, and its original earnestness with its demands. The reformation aims also at saving the consecration of the covenant in that it again takes seriously the presence of the human being. In the strife between Luther and Zwingli about the mode of the divine presence in Holy Communion the issue was also secretly that of the human presence ; Luther noticed, what Zwingli overlooked, that by a merely symbolic presence the human being is not laid hold of and claimed in the whole of his personality.

The principle of the selection of sacramental material and acts is not attacked at all by reformations ; only some sectarians lay hands on it from time to time, without succeeding in overcoming or replacing it. It looks as if the man who has passed through the discovery of the fundamentally notholy cannot any more attain to a sacred relationship with all that is in the world ; as if the reduction of the life of faith to one sphere was the necessary centre of all religion, because if this were abandoned, it would mean the removal of the bulwark against pantheism, which threatens to dissolve concrete religion. ' Existing alone ' says the South Sea singer* about his God Taaroa or Tangaroa, ' he transforms himself into world. The pivot on which the world spins round is Taaroa, he is its support. Taaroa is the sand of the original grains.' Concrete religion must fear to let the image of the Lord, the eternal counterpart in the faith relationship, run out into ' the sand of the original grains.'

There has, however, existed an essentially reformative, great religious movement which

---

* I. A. Moerenhout, *Voyages aux Iles du Grand Océan* (Paris, 1837), i. 419. (The translation given by Bastian in his *Heiligen Sage der Polynesier* is far too free.

outlined a new pansacramentalism. It did not go back behind that critical discovery, for the way there is barred, and he who attempts a return ends in madness or mere literature ; it pressed forward to a new comprehensiveness. This comprehensiveness, which is without reduction, knows that the sacramental substance cannot be found nor manipulated in the totality of things and functions, but it believes that it can be awakened and set free in each object and in each act, not by methods which somehow can be acquired, but through the all-penetrating presence of the whole man who wholly gives himself ; through sacramental existence.

The great movement, the great occurrence of which I speak, the chassidic movement, arose two centuries ago (according to legend the ' disclosing' of its founder must be set about 1735) in a dark corner of Eastern Europe, and there—degenerated, but still able to be regenerated—it remained. But the movement must be taken up into the history of religion as an incomparable attempt to rescue the sacramental life of man from being killed by facile routine.

To chassidic pansacramentalism the holy in things is not, as it is to primitive pansacramentalism, a force which one takes possession of, a power which one can overpower, but it is laid on the things, laid in them as sparks, and waits for its disentanglement and fulfilment through the human being who offers himself completely. The man of sacramental existence is not a magician ; he does not merely put himself at stake on it ; he exercises no power, but a service, the service ; he offers himself really and unreservedly. He gives himself up in service, always. To the question what is important in a sacramental sense, the answer is, ' That with which one is immediately occupied '. When, however, each case is taken seriously in its individuality, in its character of the only one, of the approaching situation, it proves itself to be that which cannot be anticipated, which is withdrawn from planning and precautionary measures. No acquired formulae and rhythms of any kind, no inherited methods of exercising power, nothing which can be known, nothing which can be learnt, are of any use to the man of sacramental existence ; he has ever to endure through the moment which cannot be speired out beforehand, where foresight is of no avail, ever to hold out to each thing or being redemption, fulfilment in the moment which rushes towards him. And he cannot begin to select, to divide ; for it is not for him to decide what shall meet him and what shall not meet him ; and there is, moreover, no not-holy, there is only that which has not yet been hallowed, which has not yet been redeemed to its holiness, that which he shall hallow.

The chassidic movement is usually taken to be a revolt of ' feeling ' against a religious rationalism which overintensified and froze the teaching of the divine transcendence, and against a ritualism which made the practice of fulfilling the Law independent and prosaic. But what is given in this antithesis cannot be understood by means of the conception of feeling ; it is the sudden rise of a true vision of unity, and of a passionate demand for wholeness. It is not merely a repressed emotional life which demands its rights that here stands over against its opponent ; it is much more an image of God which has grown greater, and a will to reality which has grown stronger. The frontier-line drawn between God and world in teaching, and the frontier-line drawn between the holy and the profane in life, satisfy no longer that double insight which has grown up, because both frontier-lines are static, immovable, unrooted in time, because they do not admit of any influence from what really happens

in time. The enhanced image of God demands a
more dynamic, a more fluid frontier between God
and world, for it has knowledge of a power that
desires to diffuse itself, and which yet limits itself,
of an opposing and yet also yielding substance.
And the strengthened will to reality demands a
more dynamic, more fluid frontier-line between the
provinces of what is holy and what is profane, for
it is not able to leave the redemption, against which
is promised that both provinces shall become one,
to its relative, the messianic time ; it must actively
desire that the moment shall ever receive what
rightfully falls to it.    Above all, it must be
observed, from a purely historical point of view,
that already inside that ' rabbinic ' world around
which the battle raged were all the elements of the
' new ', fighting for domination, and gaining
ground.    In order to understand this, it is necessary to know, what has been all too little acknowledged, that a tendency towards sacramental life
has always been powerful within Judaism.    It can
be proved against other conceptions that there is
scarcely any one Christian sacrament which has
not a sacramental or semi-sacramental Jewish
pattern ; this, however, is not of decisive importance in this connection, but what is of importance
is that at all times, also during the talmudic period,
masters of unmistakably sacramental forms of
existence arose, men then in whose lives and in
whose whole attitude to life, in whose experiences
and acts, the consecration of the covenant showed
itself effectively.    The historical line of such
people is well-nigh unbroken.    The ' zaddik ' of
the dawn of Chassidism, the classical zaddik, is
only a specially clear-cut, theoretically delineated
example of the same *ur*-type as has come down to
us from the biblical world and points into a future
world.
    The chassidic pansacramentalism can, however,

be grasped on a still more important level of being
when one considers the relationship of the movement to the Kabbalah.*   Chassidism did not fight
the Kabbalah as it fought rabbinism ;  it wanted to
continue and perfect the Kabbalah ;  it has taken
over its conceptual world, frequently its style, on
some points also the methodology of its teaching ;
and kabbalistic works by chassidic writers do not
depart from the beaten track of the later Kabbalah.
Also theurgical practices of kabbalistic stamp make
their appearance more than once in the history of
Chassidism, sometimes in strangely anarchonistic
ways.   Nevertheless, in its own nature, it breaks
with the fundamental principles of the Kabbalah ;
where it is concerned with its true object, with the
life lived in the covenant, it speaks with a quite
different voice, and on essential points it speaks in
opposition to the kabbalistic teaching and attitude,
nowhere explicitly, perhaps nowhere consciously,
but yet unmistakably ;  and what counts still more:
In a legendary literature, whose like for size, many-
sidedness, vitality, and indigenous wild charm I
do not know, it knows to tell of its central men, of
all the many zaddikim ;  that gives almost throughout a quite different being, a quite different existence as that of Kabbalism, open to the world,
pious in its attitude to the world, in love with the
world.

   First, an antithesis which seems to be superficial but which is significant, the Kabbalah is
esoteric.  What it says hides something unsaid.
The ultimate meaning is only open to the adepts,
to the initiated.   A cleft runs also through humanity with respect to the approach to God's reality.
That Chassidism cannot tolerate :  *Here*, at the
approach, there must not be any more differentiation, here holds the brotherhood of the Father's

---

* The standard synoptic work on the Kabbalah is the article of this
name by Gerhard Scholem in the *Encyclopaedia Judaica*, ix. 630-751.

sons, the secret is for all or none, to none or to all is the heart of eternity open. What is reserved for the learned part of mankind, what is kept from the poor in spirit, cannot be the living truth. Chassidic legend praises in bold, love-filled tones the simple man. He has an undivided soul; where there is a union of the soul, there will God's unity dwell. Sacramental union means the life of the unity with the unity.

The Kabbalah is according to its origin, but also according to the nature which always breaks forth, a gnosis, and, moreover, in distinction from all other gnoses, an anti-dualistic gnosis.*

To express it with the simplification necessary in this connection: The origin of all gnosis is the *ur*-question which has been pressed till one despairs of the world, the question: How is the contradiction which in the course of each life and of each history is experienced as insuperable, the biting essence of existence in this world, how is this to be reconciled with God's existence? This pressing of the question is later than the Old Testament; each true gnosis arises in a cultural environment which has been touched by the Old Testament, almost each gnosis is explicitly or implicitly a revolt against it. The biblical experience of unity— One determining power, One superior partner of man—meets the experience of contradiction that comes from depths of suffering by pointing to the mysticism of the secret: To determine what that is which appears as contradiction or absurdity is an insurmountable barrier for knowledge (Job), but is dimly to be conceived in the lived through mystery of suffering (Deutero-Isaiah); exactly

---

* When the important book by Hans Jonas, *Gnosis und spatantiker Geist* (first volume, 1934) is published in full, it will probably be proved that the teaching of Plotinus should also be regarded as a predominantly anti-dualistic reform of gnosis; but it can then only still be regarded as a transformation of gnosis into philosophy, not, like the Kabbalah, as gnosis.

here emerges the strongest manifestation of sacramental existence, in which the suffering itself becomes a sacrament (*Isaiah*, ch. 53). But the
Jewish apocalyptic literature cannot any longer
grasp the question; the *Apocalypse of Esdras*
(' The Fourth Book of Esdras '), for instance, does
not know any longer of the trusting intercourse
with the secret, but retains only the submission
without nearness, which is, at the same time, the
renunciation of the world and the spoliation of the
sacramental life. It is at this point that gnosis
intervenes, only just employing the stones from the
tumbled-down, huge, edifices of ancient, oriental
religions to build up the most fantastic new structure. It interprets the problematic of the world
as a problematic of the deity, be it that a negative
principle, evil or only bad, stands over against the
good God, be it that brittle or corruptible powers
spring from the good itself, powers which fall
into the sphere of evil, and as world-soul bear the
destiny of the contradiction, until they are allowed
to ascend again. In these conceptions the other is
always taken for granted, the antagonistic or
merely resisting force, the counter-power or the
counter-world, and it is described more or less
massively, sometimes even only as ' the place of
shadows and emptiness ' (Valentin). The undertaking of the Kabbalah was to deprive this other of
its independence, and draw even it into the dynamic
of the divine unity. By using a combination of
gnostic and neo-platonic schemata the Kabbalah
fashioned a monstrous prodigy of talmudic teaching. It is the teaching which stood up against the
apocalyptic resignation, the teaching about the
divine attributes or qualities of severity and mercy
and their dialectic intercourse, in which the drama
of the world process appears as a drama falling
within the deity. This dual dialectic, which it is
important to grasp as real, and yet not dualistic,

is multiplied by the Kabbalah in the intercourse of
the ' sefiroth ', the divine *ur*-numbers or *ur*-
glories with each other, the powers and orders
which it lets proceed from the eternally hidden
aseity of God, called the ' Without End ', through
a ' contraction ' and a ' division ' remaining in God
and yet founding the world. Their progressively
descending arrangement continues into the world's
layers, till the lowest, corporeal world of ' shells '
is reached ; the dynamic of their covering and
uncovering, their pouring forth and damming up,
their binding and loosening, produce the problematic of the cosmic and creaturely existence. As
the pre-cosmic catastrophies of 'the Death of the
*Ur*-Kings, or ' the Splintering of the Vessels' with
their cosmic consequences arose out of separations,
dislocations of gravity, sudden floods in the domain
of the aeons, so have also all inner-worldly hind-
rances and perturbations arisen down to those
demonic powers which befall the human soul.
And yet it is just from this our world that the conquest of the problematic can be effected, through
the sacramental act of man who by prayer and act
aims at the supreme secrets of the names of God
and their intertwining ; through this is the service
rendered towards the union of the powers of God,
in which the second union, the perfect unity of
being, prepares itself. Also the kabbalistic reconciliation of the experience of unity and the experience of contradiction is ultimately, like the biblical
reconciliation, a sacramental one.

But the protest against the Kabbalah announces
itself twice in Chassidism ; it is not spoken out
loud, but it is strong in its actual foundation on
facts.

The one protest directs itself against the sche-
matising of the *mysterium*. It is for the Kabbalah,
as for all gnosis, essential to see through the
contradiction of existence and to free itself from

it ; it is essential for Chassidism trustfully to
endure the contradiction and thus redeem it. The
Kabbalah makes a sketch-map of the *ur*-secrets,
on which also the springs of the contradictions
find their place. Chassidism—in so far as it
' traffics in Kabbalah ' which it does frequently
but seldom more than peripherically—retains its
picture of the upper world, as it is not able to
substitute another picture. But it is within its
own jurisdiction agnostic, it is not concerned with
an objective knowledge which can be formulated
and schematised, it is concerned with the vital,
the biblical ' knowledge ' of the fundamental,
mutual relationship to God. It is true that ' just
the classical masters of the Kabbalah always contested that the unfolding into mortal things of the
goodness laid up in God which is presented in their
teachings connecting theology and cosmogony till
the two become indistinguishable, should be an
objective process, that is, a process as it appears
from the side of God '.* But this is only a metaphysical and epistemological principle which clings
to the outside of the system and does not tend towards practice ; it does not enter into the system
itself at any point ; the whole systematic structure
of the Kabbalah is determined by a principle of
certitude which almost never stops short, almost
never cowers with terror, almost never prostrates
itself. Chassidic piety, on the other hand, finds
its real life just in stopping short, in letting itself
be disconcerted, in its deep-seated knowledge of
the impotence of all ready-made knowledge, of the
incongruity of all acquired truth, in the ' holy
uncertainty.' In this is also founded its love of
those ' lacking in knowing '. What is of importance ? A man may ' climb about in the upper
worlds ' ; suddenly it touches him, and everything

* Scholem, *op. cit.*, p. 670.

is in confusion, and he stands in an infinite, pathless darkness before the eternal presence. Only the defenceless, outstretched hand of him who is uncertain is not withered by the lightning. We are sent into the world of contradiction; when we soar away from it into spheres where it appears transparent to us, then we evade our task. It would be contrary to the trust and humour of our existence—Chassidism is both trustful and humorous—to believe that there is a stratum of existence into which we only need to raise ourselves to get ' behind ' the problematic. The absurd has been given me that I may sustain and carry it out in my life ; to sustain and carry out the absurd is the meaning which I can experience.

The second chassidic protest against the Kabbalah turns on its making the *mysterium* into magic. Magic is not at all identical with faith in man's influence beyond himself, that is, in the effect human nature and human life have on the thither side of what can be understood from the point of view of the logic of causality ; magic is rather the conviction within this faith that there are definite inner and outer acts and attitudes which can be handed down and are handed down, and through the execution of which the believed effect is reached. Magic can exist both inside and outside sacramentalism, and in the cases where it appears in connection with gnosis it is simply its other side ; its capacity to survey the means, and now these means are the means to be employed against the contradiction of existence, belongs together with the gnostic transparency of the contradiction. These traditional, magic methods could be used in the Kabbalah in connection with very different activities in life ; they are the ' kawanoth ', the intentions which were created out of the rich store of name- and letter-mysticism, and which, together with what they effected on letters and names, also wanted to have an effect on the natures themselves. And again, just as Chassidism preserved the kabbalistic-gnostic schemata on the outskirts of its teaching, and paid no heed to them in its central teaching, so it knows in its practice of the methods of intention, which can be learnt, yes, it knows of all kinds of kabbalistic-magical material, even to saving words and amulettes, but its character asserts itself in practical and not rarely also in authoritative declarations against it. Against the kawanoth which can be known—in this and this way one should meditate, in this and this way one should recollect oneself—rises up the one life-embracing kawanah of the man who gives himself up to God and his redeeming work. As Chassidism strove to overcome the division between the holy and the profane, so it also strove to overcome the emphasis on fixed procedures of intention among the fullness of the living deed. Man does not truly engage in kawanah when he accompanies an act with an already known mystical method, he exercises kawanah when he completes his act with the whole of his being facing towards God. What can be known beforehand is not made for giving the deed its living centre; for the sacramental act should not be accomplished with arbitrariness posing as creator, it is only done in connection with that which comes up to us, and as our counter-gesture; but we cannot know beforehand what comes to meet us, God and the moment cannot be known before they appear, and the moment is God's garment; therefore we can indeed prepare ourselves for the act, but we cannot prepare the act itself. The substance of the act is ever supplied to us, or rather, it is offered us—by that which happens to us, which meets us—by everything which meets us. Everything desires to be hallowed, to be redeemed, everything in the world in its worldliness, it does not desire to be emptied of its worldliness, it desires to be hallowed in the kawanah of redemption in all its worldliness; everything desires to be a sacrament. The creature seeks us out, the things seek us out on our ways; what comes in our way needs us for its way. 'With the board and with the bench' shall one pray*; they desire to come to us, everything desires to come to us, everything desires to come to God through us. What concern of ours are the upper worlds, if they exist! Ours is 'in this lower world, in this world of the body, to let the hidden life of God shine forth.'

The word jichud, unity or union, was taken over from the Kabbalah by Chassidism as a description of the sacramental act. The word has a threefold meaning. Originally it meant the unity of God which comprehends and bears all the manifoldness and all the many of existence. From this it came to mean the human acknowledgement of the unity in which man grasps all the powers that appear in nature, in history, and in life as radiations and refractions of the one power, and in his name tames the striving of each among them for becoming independent into loyal humility. But finally, it came to mean the act of man which establishes the union. For the Kabbalah this is the purposeful working for the bethrothal of the sefiroth. For Chassidism it is to draw all the desires and passions of a person into one unity moving towards God, a unity which stands unconditionally open to the world and hallows all things and also their very resistance within the unity; it is to offer this unity of world-tied sacramental existence to God for the work of his redeeming union, 'the union of the holy God with his world-indwelling glory.'

---

* Buber, *Die Chassidischen Bucher* (1928), p. 470.

# THE BEGINNINGS OF CHASSIDISM

## 1

THE appearance of Chassidism within the
history of faith of Judaism and its importance for the general history of religion cannot be understood on the basis of its teaching as
such. Regarded by itself the chassidic teaching
offers no new spiritual elements, it presents only
a selection, which it has taken partly from the later
Kabbalah, and partly from popular traditions
among the people. It is true that these spiritual
elements have been worked out anew, formulated
anew, shaped into a new unity ; but also the point
of reference which determined this selection is
not theoretical. The decisive factor for the nature
and greatness of Chassidism is not found in a
teaching, but in a mode of life ; and, indeed, in a
mode of life which shapes a community, and
regulates a community in accordance with its own
nature. But even here the relationship between
the teaching and the mode of life does not at all
belong to the type in which a mode of life
may be regarded as a carrying out of a teaching ;
it functions much more in the opposite direction :
It is the new mode of life which presses towards a
conceptual expression, a theological interpretation ;
and the practical point of reference, which determines the selection, has its origin in this need for
theological interpretation. It is also this relationship which accounts for the fact that the founder of
chassidic theology, Baer of Meseritch, did not call
Baalshem, the founder of the chassidic movement,
his teacher, although, as Baer himself recounts,
Baalshem had taught him secrets and ' unifications ',
the language of the birds, and the writing of the
angels ; Baalshem had no new *theologoumena* to

communicate to him, but a living relationship with this world and the upper world. Baalshem himself belongs to those central figures in the history of religion who have done their work by living in a certain way, not from out of a teaching but towards a teaching, who have lived in such a way that their life acted as a teaching, as a teaching not yet translated into words. The life of such people stands in need of a theological commentary; their own words form a contribution towards this, but often it is only a very fragmentary contribution; sometimes their words can be used only as a kind of introduction, for these words do not in any way offer elucidations, but are, in accordance with their original purpose, expressions of their speakers' lives. In the words of Baalshem which we know (as far as we can regard them as correctly handed down) the importance is not found in their objective content, which can be separated off from them, but in their character of pointing to a life. Two different things must be added to this: Firstly, that the nature of this life is given by the wholly personal mode of faith, and that this faith acts in such a way as to form a community. Let it be noted: It does not form a fraternity, it does not form a separate order, which guards an esoteric teaching, apart from public life; it forms a community, it forms a community of people; these people continue living their life within their family, rank, public activity, while the community into which they are formed binds some more closely, others more loosely, to the Master; but all these people imprint on their own, free, public life the system of life which they have received by association with the Master. The determining factor in the whole of this process is that the Master does not live alone by himself, or lead a secluded life with a group of disciples, but that he lives in the world and with the world. It is just this living in the

world and with the world which belongs to the
innermost core of his mode of faith.  Secondly,
that there arise a circle of people within the community, who lead the same kind of life, some of
whom have reached a similar mode of life independently of the Master, but who, through him,
have received the decisive stimulation, the decisive
moulding, people in different stages, of very
different natures, but all endowed with just the
one common, basic trend to carry the teaching on
by their lives, until everything they say is but a
marginal gloss on it.  Each life a life in itself, but
as such it forms the community ;  this is the life
in the world and with the world, and a life which,
again in its turn, gives birth to people of the same
kind in the spirit.  The flowering period of the
chassidic movement lasted so long as both agencies
remained active, so long as the forming of communities and the spiritual procreation of disciples
who form communities continued, that is, so long
as segregation gained no entry, and tradition was
not rent asunder ;  it lasted for about five generations
from Baalshem.  The communities were not by
any means communities of human paragons, nor
were their leaders at any time the kind of men who
would be called saints in Christianity or Buddhism,
but the communities were communities, and the
leaders were leaders.  The 'Zaddikim' of these
five generations offer us a number of religious
personalities of a vitality, a spiritual strength, a
many-sided individuality such as have never, to
my knowledge, appeared together in so short a
time-span in the history of religion.  But the most
important thing about these zaddikim is that each
of them was surrounded by a community that lived
a brotherly life, and who could live in this way
because there was a leading person in their midst
who brought each one nearer to the other by
bringing them all nearer to that in which they

believed. In a century which was, apart from this, not very productive religiously—not even in Eastern Europe—the obscure Polish and Ukrainian Jewry produced the greatest we know in the history of the spirit, something which is greater than any solitary genius in art or in the world of thought, a society which lives in its faith.

Because this is so, because Chassidism in the first instance does not signify a category of teaching, but one of living, its legend is our main source for understanding it, and only after its legend comes its theoretical literature. The theoretical literature is the gloss, the legend is the text, and that in spite of the fact that it is a legend which has been handed down in an extreme state of corruption, and which it is impossible to recover in its purity. It would be foolish to object that legend cannot transmit the reality of chassidic life. It is obvious that legend is not chronicle ; however, to him who knows how to read the legend, it conveys more truth than the chronicle. It is indeed not possible to reconstruct from it the factual course of events, but, in spite of its corruption, it is possible to contemplate in it the living elements in which the events have consummated themselves, to see them in that which was received and told with naive enthusiasm, and told till it became legend. Apart from secondary, literary elaborations, which betray themselves as such at first glance, no external will dominates these tales. Those who told these tales were driven by an inner constraint, the nature of which is the chassidic life, the pulsating, chassidic relationship of leader and community. Even the most daring miracle-stories are not usually the product of calculated invention. The zaddik had done what had never been heard of before, with unheard-of power he had laid his spell over the souls of men, they experienced his work as a miracle, they could but tell of it in the language of miracle. It used to be common further to refer to the fact that many of these tales are of much older origin ; much of what is told of the masters of the Talmud, we find here again recounted as the act of zaddikim. But even this grossly unhistorical attitude has its share of truth. The naive mind that experienced the beatific present weaved into it the tradition of the past that was in tune with the present—any thought of forgery was far from the minds of these story-tellers, for, after all, the old stories were mostly known to every one. What happened must rather be conceived of as the spontaneous rise of the rumour that the Rabbi has now done anew this or that well-known deed ; he acted in such and such a way, not in order to imitate the first doer, but completely naturally, because there are certain basic forms of good works. How, for instance, could the irrepressible eagerness to help the helpless find a more direct expression than by the Rabbi coming late to communal prayer, because he must stop on his way to quiet a weeping child ? Or how could the inner freedom as contrasted with possessions be more radically expressed than by the Rabbi declaring all that he owns to be ownerless before he goes to bed at night, so that the burden of sin may remain far from the thieves who might enter in ? However, most often one finds that something new and characteristic has come into the stories in the re-telling of them. What had been handed down was, according to its very nature, an example of the *individual* life. In the atmosphere of the *community* life it became something different.

## 2

It is only when one recalls how the sabbatinian catastrophe worked itself out in the Jewry of Poland and the Ukraine that one can understand the rise of the new principle of life which appeared in the chassidic movement. The eruption of an ever-swelling hope reached its climax a quarter of a century after the death of Sabbatai Zwi just in this part of Jewry and in spite of the great dis-illusionment caused by him, when the host of penitents led by Jakob Chassid set out on their wanderings to Palestine, wanderings which are almost reminiscent of the phenomena that were called forth by the crusades. It was in this part of Jewry that the sabbatinian disintegration of the teaching, which one rightly has called a religious nihilism, sent forth its extreme consequence in the form of the sect of Frank, truly the strangest formation of the spiritual lie in modern history. It was also in this part of Jewry that its counter-movement arose in Chassidism. By ' counter-movement ' I do not understand a movement which carries on an external fight against an outward appearance, but rather a counter-force, which arises out of the depth of the capacity of the organic community-life to build new community-cells, different in kind from the old ones, standing firm against the disintegration of the old cells and the disintegration with which this process threatens the organism, the re-birth of a healthy capacity to believe on the part of a people lying fatally sick in a perversion of its faith. From this it is easily seen to follow that the counter-movement cannot by its very nature be a reformation ; it cannot be a desire for a return to an earlier condition that had no problems, to the condition which obtained before the illness supervened. The counter-move-ment takes for its beginning the given conflict of elements as they exist in the present, and then it distils the antidote from the very same material as the inner poison used for its own brew. It is not without significance in this connection that the decisive development of Chassidism did not occur after the movement of Frank, but simultaneously with it.

It is to the work of G. Scholem that we owe that knowledge and understanding of the sabbatinian theology which now make it possible for us to grasp the dialectic of the post-sabbatinian, spiritual history in its movement and counter-movement. We knew the uncanny, historical fact of Sabbatai Zwi, the appearance of this messianic pretender whom the masses received with a jubilant ' yes ' after all the ' no's ' that generations of men waiting for the Messiah had given to all his predecessors ; we knew of him, how he then, crowned and worshipped as the holy King, left Judaism. But now we also know the still more uncanny theology that was familiar with all the artifices with which gnosticism perverts value, and which used them to re-interpret the meaning of the event till it became its opposite : The conception of the Messiah as he who must enter completely into the ' Klipah ', the daemonic power of the shells, that he may liberate the holiness there held fast, and who in doing thus fulfils the purpose of the exile of Israel, and redeems Israel and the world in one. But even that is not enough: The holy sin becomes a pattern, men must hurl themselves into sin in order to tear from it the holy sparks ; and soon there is no sin any longer, with the fulfilment of the meaning of the new, messianic aeon the yoke of the old Torah has been broken ; it was only valid for the unredeemed world, and now the new revelation has come ; the revelation which allows all and hallows all is here.

It is obvious that the sabbatinian theology is the climax of the process which began in kabbalistic eschatology, where messianism was being made an alien thing through its being impregnated with gnosis. In the faith of the prophets the Messiah was the perfect man, who came forth from Israel, and who, as God's vicegerent, did the work that had been reserved for man to do. We find as late as in a Jewish-Christian gospel the conception of a God who ' in all the prophets ' ' expects ' him who shall come. It is in this dramatic confrontation of God and man that the faith of Israel is rooted, and it is this confrontation which first in the apocalyptic literature and then later in the Kabbalah becomes more and more obliterated ; divine emanations mediate between heaven and earth, it is one of these who descends to the world of men as the Messiah, and finally Sabbatai Zwi is prayed to as ' the true God and King of the World '. It is only logically consistent that he, like the gnostic Christ, journeys to the hell of this world, and makes himself like unto its rulers in order to lead them captive. But though it was from the later Kabbalah that the sabbatinian theology took its conception of the holy sparks which are to be drawn forth from out of the uncleanness, the conception itself is in the last resort not of syncretistic but of Jewish origin. That the togetherness of man with God, with God who ' yet dwells with them in the midst of their uncleanness ', purifies and hallows all ; that man must also serve God with the evil drive ; that the redemption overcomes the division between clean and unclean, holy and profane ; that *all* becomes pure and holy— this we must regard as an autotochtonous possession of the Jewish faith. The ingredients for the antidote are prepared.

The sabbatinian theology has anticipated the redeemed world, it has declared for present use the draft on a reality which is to come into being only in a perfection of the world which is still beyond ken. In doing this it undermined the Torah, and bereft it of its living substance, for Torah is only firm and alive so long as man is shown a way as the way of God ; to guide a man on his way means to give him guidance for an existence which is within his ken, and it always implies exclusion of all that which is not the way for him.  It is only within the context of the messianic expectation and preparation that one can rightly lay hold of the fact that in a world of perfection *all* becomes the way ;  when one treats it as an accomplished fact, and is at the same time surrounded by the facts of an unredeemed world, facts that are mightier than all theology, then one has really taken one's stand on zero, on *nihil*, and is soon done for, if one remains honest.  But from this point a two-fold possibility reveals itself :  The one can be accomplished by the complete lie, with juggling gestures it moves in the tintinnabulum of nothing as if it were something.  The other is possible for him who stakes something, namely, a new mode of life.  Both Jakob Frank and Baalshem start with the post-sabbatinian situation, behind which it is not possible to go.  The one smashes the undermined Torah, the other fills it with life.

# 3

When I say ' the complete lie ', then I do not by any means wish to imply that one can understand Frank, when one takes him to be an impostor, for that would be a misleading simplification.  By ' lie ' I do not here mean something which the human being does or says, but rather what he is. This man is not a liar, he is the lie.  This means, therefore, that he does believe himself, but after the manner of the lie, as the lie believes in itself— for also the lie has a method by which it believes in itself.  It is obvious that Sabbatai believed in something unconditioned, and that he believed in himself in relation to it ;  his ' messianic consciousness ' was based on this.  It is not the belief as such, but the belief in himself, which does not

stand firm ; when later a compromise between both
types of belief is set up, nothing is altered in the
fact that the ring has snapped in the decisive
moment : Sabbatai has not decided to pay for the
possibility of miracle with the possibility of martyrdom. Frank, who did not grow up in an atmosphere
of ascetic longing for redemption, as Sabbatai did,
but on the contrary in an atmosphere of libertinian
marrano environment, cannot in any way fall like
Sabbatai, because he never stood like Sabbatai ;
his public activity does not end with his secession,
it rather begins with it. Frank does not believe
in something unconditioned and in himself in
relation to it, he believes in nothing, he is not even
capable of really believing in himself, he can only
believe in himself after the manner of the lie by
filling the space of the nothing with himself. True,
for appearance's sake he populates the nothing
with divine forms, the spawn of late-gnostic
phantasy, like the Three who lead the world, and
the obscure ' Big Brother ' who is unknown even
to them. It is, however, evident that he only
plays with this world of mythology ; in reality he
holds to nothing but to himself, and he is capable
of holding to himself by himself without having
any foothold. Therefore he has nothing which
can restrain him any longer, and his freedom from
all restraint acts like a magic with which he works
on people, on those people whom he wants to
affect. When one treats of Frank, the question
does not arise whether he was mentally ill or
healthy ; he possesses real delusion, the delusion
that makes for complete lack of restraint ; he
utilises, however, this real delusion for working
magically on human beings—and he utilises his
magical, compelling effect on them not merely for
his ephemeral purposes, he comes to use it more
and more, because the nihilistic belief in himself
must draw its nourishment from outside beliefs,

when it is threatened by the crisis of self-reflection, or else it would cease to exist. When to win back his waning power Frank sends word to his adherents in Poland from the town of Offenbach that Jakob, the true and living God, lives and will live for ever, then this craving for being believed so that he himself may believe has been raised to its highest potentiality. As Israel's messianism was done away with in Sabbatinianism, so here the sabbatinian, emanational messianism does away with itself: Neither God nor his emanation exists any longer, there is left only the human person who fills the nothing. But if the human being who conceives of himself as this person is to continue to do so, he must unceasingly absorb into himself the warm flesh and blood of external belief in him. The group of disciples that gather round him, and allow themselves to be thus absorbed by him, with their orgies and raptures, form the daemonic community of the daemonic Messiah; in the midst of the Christian Church they advertise the decay of the community of Israel. The sabbatinian torrent had overwhelmed the strong life of the Jewish community, and from the flood there emerges its caricature, the anti-community. This crowd is without any restraints, and yet, at the same time, it is utterly tied to a leader who leads it into nothing; thus it affords an unsurpassable spectacle of disintegration.

4

Just like Frankism so Chassidism starts from the situation which was created by the sabbatinian disaster, but, unlike Frankism, Chassidism does not do so in order to go further. There is no going further unless it be to corruption and decay. Chassidism recognises the disaster which has happened as a disaster, not only as a disaster within

the nation and belonging to the inner world, but
as a disaster in the relationship between God and
Israel, between God and men.  The relation between deity and mankind has suffered a grave
injury, the apparently intimate nearness between
them has revealed itself to be misuse ; what appeared as mandate ended in treachery.  The
injury done to the relationship between the upper
and lower worlds continues to increase, the lie
becomes mighty, and poses as the new truth.  It
threatens not only to enmesh the utterly bewildered,
unstable Jewry in madness and guilt ; it threatens
to undermine not only the inner and outer structure
of Jewry, but it threatens to create a breach between it and God, a deeper fissure than any that
has ever been.  It is at this point that the new
element takes hold in the form of the mode of life of
Baalshem and of those who belong to him.  The
question is no longer that of the healing of the
people, but a question of healing the broken
relationship between heaven and earth.  The evil
must be checked, before it becomes invincible.
And that cannot be done by fighting ; it can only
be effected through new mediation and new
guidance.

It is no accident that the new movement arose
in Podolia.  From the days of Sabbatai Zwi till
the time of the birth of Baalshem, Podolia had
belonged to Turkey, and it was Turkish Jewry that
had been specially exposed to the problems of the
post-sabbatinian period ; it was also here that
Frank had first gained a foothold.  Baalshem is to
be understood on the background of this people
who had been shaken by the feverish character of
the two movements, and who were still shivering
in the ague of its deepest night.  The solitude in
which Baalshem spent his youth amidst the stillness of the Carpathian mountains symbolises the
gathering strength to withstand the seduction.

When he came forth, it was to work for the healing of body and soul. A story, which is characteristic for his work, is given by the legend which tells of how he won the Great Maggid, the man who was destined to complete his teaching: First Baalshem helps the Great Maggid to conquer a physical illness ; next Baalshem shows him that his knowledge is no knowledge, and then follows a manifestation which comes upon the recipient as a vision-like event, and shakes his innermost soul. Baalshem's real work is this winning of people for a new mode of life, it is the building up of a community of people who are both rejoicing in the world and orientated towards the nearness of God, a community that is scattered throughout the country, and which yet, nevertheless, forms a circle round him. During the latter part of his life, and after his death, it was this work which stood out against the behaviour of Frank's adherents. It is said that Baalshem took part in the rabbinical disputations against the sect ; this, however, is not only historically false, but also untrue to his nature. His true attitude is shown by the following story: Once, on the Eve of the Day of Atonement, he was so overwhelmed by the thought of the danger that threatened Israel in that it might lose its organic connection with tradition together with the Oral Torah that he had to break off in the middle of the blessing of the community ; he threw himself down before the Ark, and accused the rabbis of not having rightly guarded the wealth entrusted to them ; during the final prayer on the following day he was translated to the gate of heaven, and there he found the prayers that had failed to gain entrance into heaven during the last fifty years ; he went and sought out the Messiah, and with his help he succeeded in gaining an entrance together with the prayers, and the impending fate was averted amidst the rejoicing of heaven. The important point in this story is that the prayers of the last fifty years had to wait on earth, until they were raised up to the gate of heaven on this Day of Atonement by the powerful prayers of the community of Baalshem. From this it follows that the prayers of the rabbinic community could not mount to heaven by themselves during the sabbatinian period, and had to be raised up by the new movement. It was in fact not only against the movement of Frank that Baalshem took a stand by his life and teaching, but also against the rabbinism of the time ; he accuses the latter of divorcing the Torah from real life and thus removing the people from the nearness of God ; in doing so rabbinism prepared the people for accepting the false message of God's nearness. Baalshem died soon after the mass-baptism of Frank's adherents. It is told how shortly before his death he grieved over ' the severed members of the shekhinah, the world-indwelling glory.' Legend has it that he had to die in consequence of the venture in which he took heaven by storm.

We shall, however, understand the relation between Baalshem and Sabbatinianism still better, if we consider the allusions in the story of the temptation that came close to him from that quarter. The story is told in a strangely reticent way, and it is obvious that it keeps silent about much of importance ; it recounts how Sabbatai Zwi once appeared to Baalshem to ask him for redemption. In order to effect this type of re-demption it is necessary to bind all the elements of one's own nature to those of the dead person, as Elisha brought all of his into contact with those of the dead boy ; it is necessary to join each of the three elements of one's own soul—the breath of life, the spirit, the soul itself—to those of the person who needs redemption. Baalshem wanted to fulfil the request ; however, as he feared the influence of so intimate a contact with what is evil, he was circumspect, when he began the work, and decided not to do it all at once, but to spread it over a period of time. During this time Sabbatai appeared to him once while he was asleep, and, obviously relying on the intimacy that had been established between them, he tried to tempt Baalshem. The account does not say to what he tried to tempt him, but it is not difficult to fill in the suppressed point : The false Messiah wanted to tempt Baalshem to regard himself as the Messiah and to proclaim himself as such. Baalshem, however, withstood him, and hurled him away with such force that he tumbled headlong down to the bottom of the nether world. Afterwards Baalshem used to say of him that there had been a holy spark in him, but that Satan had caught him in his coil, the coil of pride. In connection with this story one should also remember that Baalshem used to say that when one stretches one's feet out before drawing the last breath, one must not have any self-contentment, and that, according to tradition, he was heard whispering softly to himself before his death this verse from the Psalm : ' Let not the foot of pride come near me '.

When Spengler, the well-known historiosoph, wished to see in Baalshem a type of Messiah, he did so by referring to my work. But this view of Baalshem is at variance both with his self-consciousness and with his whole mode of life. There is nothing eschatological about him, there is nothing which voices any claim to be final and determining. Legend represents Baalshem as experiencing in diverse events the fact that his hour is not the hour of redemption, but the hour of renewal ; but also these stories never tell of him as behaving as the One, the Consummator; he is presented only as trying to help in the redemption, to prepare for it, and even this he does in vain. Once legend gives an indication that when the Messiah comes, then he will

prove to be him, the returning Israel Ben Eliezer.
But in this present life his nature is different, and
his task is different. Everything in him and about
him is against 'the hurrying of the End', which has
degenerated into madness and lie, and which has
brought man's relationship with God into extreme
danger by a frenzied devotion to unreal gods.
Everything points to the necessity for returning to
a beginning, to the beginning of a real life for the
real God in the real world.

## 5

It is usual to take the so-called Zaddikism to be
a later degeneration within Chassidism. But what
one calls Zaddikism is only the exaggeration of an
element which manifested itself already in the
earliest stages of Chassidism, and which cannot be
isolated from its fundamental life and teaching.

Chassidism found the conception of the zaddik
lying ready to its hand both in kabbalistic literature
and in popular tradition ; but Chassidism filled
this conception with new meaning. Both in
literature and in tradition the zaddik was taken to
be a man who was connected with God in a special
way, and who therefore not only saw into his
secrets, but also acted with full power committed
to him. In Chassidism the zaddik becomes also
the man who leads the community in God's stead,
and who mediates between God and the community.
In this context community is always taken to mean
both the special, well-defined community that is
gathered round an individual zaddik, and the community of all Israel. The latter manifests itself in
the former, the individual community is the whole
people. This development in the conception of the
zaddik by which the special position of one man
becomes an institution can again only be understood on the background of the crisis. The more

acute the crisis became, the more intense became
the quest for new leadership. In spite of various
energetic sallies the old rabbinic leadership had not
been able to overcome the crisis, for it fought only
to maintain the teaching, and not for a renewal of
life. Already from the start of the chassidic movement had chassidic circles regarded the rabbinic
leadership much in the same way as a nation regards
a government which has failed to prepare defences
against an enemy invasion, and therefore cannot
offer resistance when the invasion comes; a counter-
government has to be established. By the nature
of the case this meant that in the chassidic form of his
position, the zaddik could not any longer be primarily
a scholar. It is true that the founders of the
chassidic movement were very eager to draw outstanding talmudic scholars into their circle ; but
each of them was subjected to a searching criticism
of his former mode of life, which, together with his
induction to the different mode of life, resulted
in an inner change, which was so great that all that
had hitherto formed the centre of his existence
now became peripherical, while the new service
forms the centre of his new life. A good example
of this is afforded by the legend of Baer of
Mezirici in the house of Baalshem. This new
service is one of the strongest fusions of communion with God and communion with man known
to the history of religion. Man serves God by
helping God's creation, man helps God's creation
by leading it to God, a leading which does not
turn its back on life, but walks through the middle
of life itself. It was an education for leadership
to be a disciple in the house of the founders of the
movement.

The sabbatinian revolution had stirred the
Polish Jew in the innermost core of his being,
its end had shaken the very foundations of all that
was his world, and now he asked passionately for

leadership, he craved for a man who would take him under his wings, give certainty to his bewildered soul, order and form to an existence which had become chaotic, and who would, above all, enable him again both to believe and to live. The chassidic movement educated such leaders. Rabbis who only imparted information of how to practise the precepts of the Law did not suffice for the new demands, and sermons on the meaning of the teaching were of no use. In a world in which one could not any longer muster the necessary strength for reflection and decision, one needed a man who could show one what to believe, and who could tell one what to do. When we consider the unconditioned self-surrender of the Frankists to Frank, we can see how completely people let themselves be absorbed by a man who was prepared to shoulder all responsibility for them. The chassidic movement had to start from this. It had to produce men who would lift on to their strong shoulders all those who wanted to be carried, and who would also set them down on the ground again as soon as they could be trusted to walk by themselves. In complete contrast to the pseudo-messianic types the chassidic leaders undertook responsibility for the souls entrusted to them, while at the same time they kept alive in them the spark of responsibility. While Frank wanted people to take him to be the fulfilment that superseded the Torah, the highest praise one could give a zaddik was to say that he was a Torah, by which one meant that the part of the Torah which cannot be expressed in words, but which yet can be handed on through human existence, manifested itself in his nature, in his everyday behaviour, in his unemphatic, involuntary, unintentional acts and attitudes, in ' how he binds and loosens his sandals '. These men mediated between God and man, but at the same time they insisted on the importance of the immediate relationship to God, which cannot be replaced by any mediation.

A further, important characteristic of chassidic Zaddikism lies in the number of the zaddikim. The messianic pretender is by his very nature one single person ; zaddikhood must, by its very nature, present itself in a number of contemporaneous men, to each of whom the various parts of the community may be said to be allocated. According to a saying ascribed to Baalshem there are thirty-six hidden as well as thirty-six manifest zaddikim. In spite of all exaggeration no zaddik considers himself to be the only one ; in spite of all strife between this and that community, and all jealousy between their respective teachers and disciples, this allocation remains valid and unshaken. It is true that sometimes the chassidim believe and say that apart from their rabbi there is no other in the world ; but the fundamental opinion of the earliest chassidim is given by the zaddik who calls such behaviour a service to false gods. ' How then should one speak ? ' he asks, and answers, ' One should say, '' Our rabbi is the best rabbi for our needs ! '' '. In other words, each zaddik and his community are predestined for each other.

' I have come to help the whole world ', said Frank. The zaddik has to help his chassidim. But in order truly to help them, in order to bring them to God with their whole life, and not merely with a part of it, such as with their thoughts, or with their feeling, but really to bring them to God with their whole life, it is necessary for him to comprehend their whole life, from the concern for their food to the concern for the cleansing of their souls. He has not to do something definite for them ; he has to do everything for them. And because it is his duty to do everything, he must be able to do everything. ' Why ', it is asked jokingly, ' does one call the zaddik " the good Jew " ?  If one wanted to say that he prays well, then one would have to call him " the good prayer-ful man " ; if one wanted to say that he learns well, then " the good learner ".  " A good Jew " is good in his thinking, good in his drinking, good in his eating, good in his work, good in his intentions, and good in everything '.

The legend of Baalshem allegorises the organic connection between the zaddik and his community by making him dance with his chassidim, or by telling how when he spoke in their congregation each single one of them felt his speech as directed to him, and found in it advice for his own individual life.  But we find already the first chassidic book, which was based on sayings of Baalshem, developing a formula for this organic connection. The mutuality of the bond is emphasised in this book in the strongest possible way.  It is true that the community by itself is like the earth before it was joined with heaven, a chaos ; but ' the zad-dikim must not say that they do not need the people ', the people are like the bearers of the Ark of the Covenant without whom it cannot move, even though in reality it is the Ark that carries the bearers.  On the other hand a sharp criticism is directed against the conditions as they existed before the chassidic movement began, and as they con-tinued to exist side by side with the movement, where the learned on one side and the people on the other side presented two widely separated ' poles ', which did not enter into any relationship with each other ; the learned must become aware of their own shortcomings and take part in the life of the people, for only thus can they also lift up the masses.

# 6

But this advice should not be taken to imply that Chassidism regards ' the simple man ' as having only a passive, receptive function. On the contrary, according to chassidic views it is just with him that one can find an element of the highest active importance.

Here also we do best by starting from Frankism. Jakob Frank emphasised again and again to his adherents that he was an *am ha-aretz*, an ignorant man. ' God has chosen me ', he said, ' because I am an *am ha-aretz* '. That which is at stake is not given to the wise and the learned, but only to ' such ignorant men as I, for the wise look towards heaven, although they do not see anything there, we, however, should look on the earth '. In a beautiful picture, which among all his sayings is the one which comes nearest to the chassidic parables, he tells of the perfect pearl, which none of the masters could pierce, because non dared to do it, for each of them knew how easily he might splinter it in the process; a journeyman, who did not know the danger, undertook to pierce the pearl in the absence of his master ; and he succeeded.

The decisive difference between the world of Frank and that of Baalshem reveals itself, however, exactly at the point where they apparently come nearest to each other. Frank boasts of his ignorance, because it makes him free from all restraint. He is not bound by any knowledge of the Torah, he does not know the full divine burden of human responsibility ; it is therefore that his hand does not falter, when he pierces the pearl of the human world. He is chosen, it is not necessary for him to question the truth of what he is to do and what not to do, it is not necessary for him to decide, everything is decided. ' I have been chosen ', he

says, because I am an *am ha-aretz*, and as such I
shall with God's help pierce everything and be
brought to all '.    Later on he says no longer ' with
God's help '.    He himself is ' that burning thorn-
bush '.

The simple man, whom the chassidic teaching
praises, has not a farthing worth of self-consciousness.   He would consider himself ridiculed if told
that he was chosen.   He too has no need to decide,
for he lives his life quite simply, without any subtle
enquiries ;   he accepts the world as it is, and
wherever the opportunity comes to him, he does
the good which is entrusted to him with an un-
daunted soul, as if he had known it from all eternity ;   if, however, he once should go astray, then
he seeks with all his might for a way out, and en-
trusts his fate to God.   It is God he cares for, he is
his great Lord and Friend ;   as Lord and Friend he
addresses him continuously, he tells him everything, as if God knew nothing of it ;   he is not
embarrassed in his presence.   He can neither learn
nor pray ' rightly ', that is, use kawanoth with
secret intentions.   But he does his daily work
eagerly, and as he does it, he says the Psalms which
he knows by heart ;   also they are a way of speaking
to God, and he is sure that his speech will be
heard.   And sometimes he feels particularly glad
in his heart, and then he whistles in God's honour,
or dances and even jumps, as he cannot show him
his love in any other way.   And God rejoices over
it.   He rejoices over him.   This chassidic God
knows how to rejoice, as his chassidim know how
to rejoice.   But still more: According to legend it
sometimes happens that such a man who ' does not
know how to pray ' once opens his heart to God
with all his might in the middle of the prayer of the
community, and with the strength of his prayer he
carries up all weak and maimed prayers that have
no wings to rise.   Also he has the power to unite.

It is told of one of the chassidim, a man who was outstanding for his patience, his prayer, and his love of music, Rabbi Israel of Kosnitz, that he specially liked the ' simple people ' to come to him ; when his disciples asked him why, he said to them : ' As for me—all my travail and work are aimed at making myself simple, and they are already simple '.

And just because ' the simple man ' is so important, there cannot be any esoteric Chassidism, in contrast to the Kabbalah, so long as the movement retains its original strength and purity. There is no shutting up of the secrets ; everything is fundamentally open to all, and everything is again and again repeated so simply and concretely that each true believer can grasp it. Attention has rightly been drawn to the impetus which the chassidic movement received from its recognition of the formerly despised *am ha-aretz* as a member with equal, religious rights in the community, and from its admiration for the simply believing man. One must, however, add to this that from its beginning the movement was supported in the wider circles of the community by a new generation, yea by a new type of man, and that this type of man would not have anything more to do with the ' hurrying of the End', which was so fateful in its consequences, but that he undertook to serve God with the strength given him in each hour of his life. It must further be added that it was this type of man which the movement strove to heighten in the eyes of the people, and in doing so it attempted to enlarge the new spiritual authority of the zaddik by establishing a religious élite that arose from out of the masses themselves.

## 7

Frank had based the glorification of his own ignorance on the grounds that the earlier way, the

way of knowledge of precepts and the teachings
of faith, had now been supplanted by a new way,
' which never yet, since the beginning of the world,
had occurred to one human being '.  The old
words had been ' long'dead ', the precepts must be
' splintered like a fragment of pottery ', everything
that preceded must fall, before the new structure
is erected for eternity.  ' The Christ which is
known to you has said that he has come to deliver
the world from out of the hands of Satan, but I
have come to deliver it from all the dogmas and
ordinances which have existed hitherto.  I must
abrogate it all, and then the Good God will reveal
himself ' (that is, in accordance with the current
gnostic conception, the hidden God, who is not
identical with the creator and ruler of the world).
For this reason he demands of his adherents that
they shall ' wash themselves clean of all precepts ',
as ' the highpriest washed himself clean, before
he entered the Holy of Holies ' ;  they must doff all
the precepts and teaching of faith that cling to
them, and follow him step for step.  Once, however, he gives utterance to the statement, ' All
leaders must be without religion '.  The statement reminds one of the conviction which, according to reports, is entertained by the holder of the
highest grade within the sect of Assassins, and which
according to recently published reports, also must
be regarded as the real creed of the world-histor-
ical Assassinism of our day.

Chassidism starts also on this point from the
situation as it is given by the crisis, and does not
attempt to go behind it.  The sabbatinian anti-
nomianism had questioned the position of the
Torah as law in its traditional sense, that is as a sum
of God's commandments, which had no other
purpose than to allow men to fulfil his inscrutable
will.  The chassidic movement cannot aim at
re-instating the Torah conceived in this way.  It

can and will only preserve the Torah by sub-
stituting a floating boundary for the clear-cut
frontier-line drawn between the spheres of the per-
missible and the forbidden things on the one hand,
and the indifferent things, the ' adisphora ' on the
other hand. The chassidic conception of the
Torah is a further development of the traditional
belief that God wishes to use man in the conquest
of the world which he has created. God wills to
make it truly into his own world, his own dominion,
but only through the act of man. The intention
of the divine revelation is to form men who can
work for the redemption of the world. By this is
not meant one single, messianic act, but the deeds
of the everyday, which prepare for the messianic
fulfilment. A harmony of all functions is here
substituted for the eschatological fever of the crisis,
and this harmony does not simply mean health, it
means rather healing. The ' mizwoth ', the commandments, mark the sphere of the things which
are already expressly given over to man for sanctification. Chassidism developed the late kabbalistic
teaching of the divine sparks that have fallen into
things and which can be ' lifted up ' by man. For
such a lifting up the mizwoth are recommended
to man. He who does a mizwah with complete
kawanah, that is, completes an act in such a way
that his whole existence is gathered in it and
directed in it towards God, he works on the redemption of the world, on its conquest for God.
But the sparks which need to be raised do not only
rest in the things referred to by the mizwoth.
The demarcation between that which is holy, that
is, that which has been appointed for sanctification,
and that which is profane, that is that which lacks
such a specific reference, is a provisional one.
The Torah marks the past circumference of
revelation. It depends on man whether and to
what an extent this expands. ' Why ', asks a

zaddik, ' do we speak of " the time when the Torah *has been* given " and not of " the time when the Torah *was* given " ? God wills that all should be hallowed, until in the messianic time there will be no more division between what is holy and what is profane, because everything has become holy '. Here again Chassidism has reached a position which is apparently in the closest proximity to that of sabbatinian theology ; it cannot be different, as Chassidism conscienteously starts from the situation that bears the imprint of Sabbatinianism ; here again we see the unconditional opposition of Chassidism to Sabbatinianism. The removal of the wall of partition between permitted and forbidden will not take place in the messianic hour, and thus supersede the Torah, but rather the messianic hour will mark the completion of the work by which all things and all life are penetrated by hallowing, and the Torah, which has become whole and entire, will include the whole of life ; indeed, there will not any longer exist anything except the existence into which the Torah has entered, and in which it has come to life. A saying from the early time of Chassidism glosses the text, ' Be holy, for I, JHWH, your God, am holy ' by remarking ' now the holiness of Israel comes from the mizwoth, as it is said in the prayer, " as you have hallowed us through your commandments ", but in the future of which the talmudic teaching promises us that the mizwoth will be lifted, the holiness of Israel will come immediately from the holiness of God '. And a later saying draws the conclusion of this in a comment on the text of Scripture which warns the people from ' making carved work, figure of all that which JHWH your God commanded you ' : ' Why ', asks the comment, ' does it say " commanded " and not " forbade " ? ' And the answer is, ' because one should not make for oneself any idol of a mizwah, because seen in the light of the kingdom of God every mizwah is not final '. On the other hand, there is no thing and no event of which I could say that it is not that which should be hallowed by me ; at this stage of the reality of faith there is nothing which can any longer be found to be indifferent. As the religious acceptance of the *am ha-aretz* had overcome the traditional hierarchy of persons, so through the religious acceptance of the adisphora the traditional hierarchy of acts was overcome. Also the kawanoth of prayer that had been elaborated by the later Kabbalah for the unification of God and his shekhinah retreated before him who, as one of the greatest thinkers of Chassidism said about himself, ' prays with the board and the bench '. The great kawanah does not ally itself with any selection of what has been prescribed ; everything which is done with that can be the right, the redeeming act. Each act may be the one on which it depends ; the determining factor lies in the strength and concentration with which I do the hallowing. To the question of what had been the essential point in the life of his late teacher, a disciple answered, ' Just that which he dealt with at the moment '.

## 8

Jakob Frank used to say of his star, the star which according to the prophecy of Balaam which he loved to quote, ' appeared out of Jacob ', that all contemned and common things were in the power of this star, and only to the extent to which one completely gave oneself could one attain to redemption. In order to ascend the ladder of Jacob, which consists of two sloping ladders meeting on earth, one must first descend to its very base, before one can ascend. It is necessary to make ' the alien fire ', the fire of 'sin', so one's

own that one can offer it to God ; the fire which the
sons of Aaron offered is nothing in comparison with
what one has to do at the bottom of the ladder.
Therefore one must completely and wholly enter
into Edom, where ' the alien acts ' prevail (a
description which is often found with the sab-
batinians), not secretly as in Israel, but publicly ;
Jacob must not rest satisfied as he has done before
with following in the footsteps of Esau, he must
become one life with him. Esau or Edom must
here be taken both in a literal and in a symbolic
sense ; in a literal sense, as when Frank expounded
it by the mass-baptism of his adherents and through
their apologetics ; in a symbolic sense it stands for
the dominion of sin, into which one must penetrate
most deeply in order to conquer it ; one must, as
the sabbatinian saying has it, conquer the klipah
in its house, one must fill the uncleanness with the
strength of holiness, until it breaks down from
inside. The great fortress, as Frank expresses it
in a characteristic simile, cannot be taken by all
the arts and crafts of siege, until an *am ha-aretz* at
night sneaks in through a sewer, and seizes it.

The teaching of Frank about ' the alien acts '
has its parallel in the chassidic teaching of 'the
alien thoughts '. Here also Chassidism starts from
the same presuppositions as Sabbatinianism, presuppositions which are common to both movements. The abyss is broken open ; it would be
fatal for any man to live as if the evil did not exist.
One cannot serve God by merely avoiding evil ;
one must grapple with it. The decisive difference
lies in the fact that Chassidism has the insight
to see that the breaking open of ' the shells ' is not
at an end with this occupation, but has to be begun
again and again. The sparks of the light of God
yearn for release from their deepest exile in that
which we call evil. They come to us laden with
the shells from which they cannot separate them-

selves ; they come to us as ' alien thoughts ', as
desires at all times, also during the time of prayer ;
indeed they come specially during the time of
prayer, for they act always in common with the
klipoth, as they must. The klipoth have never so
great a desire to make us fall as when we pray and
cleave to God, and the sparks of holiness demand
never so much our deed as during the time of
prayer, because then our strength is at its greatest.
But the fulfilment of their demand cannot happen
in any other way than in the form of the klipah, in
the form of temptation, in other words, in our
imaginative faculty. The old word that the greater
a person is the greater is his desire becomes modified: From the greatness of a temptation a soul
knows how holy it is in the root of its being. Imagination is the power in us which is connected
with the appearance of the sparks ; and as this
appearance comes from the blending of good and
evil, it may be said about it that it is the tree of the
knowledge of good and evil. It is here that the
decision takes place in each human being, and it is
on this decision that the redemption depends.
Therefore we should not push the alien thoughts
away from us as something annoying and noisome,
and thus repudiate the holy sparks. Their appearance is after all an appearance of God in the things
which are seemingly furthest from him, as it is
written (*Jeremiah*, 31,2) : ' From afar has JHWH
appeared unto me '. We should willingly receive
this appearance, and do that which it demands of
us: In the sphere of our imagination we should
set free the pure passion from the object which
limits it, and direct it to the limitless ; in doing so
we break the shells, and redeem the sparks which
were bound in it. It is true that a man who in this
way concerns himself with evil runs into great
danger, and many zaddikim have issued the caution
that it is reserved for holy people to go through this

hazard. But it is held up against these zaddikim
that each man is in the world in order to work on
the cleansing and liberation of the world ; in order
to withstand the danger he should daily judge
himself : In the fire of such a judgement the
innermost heart becomes ever stronger, and the
power of the klipah cannot touch it.

Here, in the dominion of ' the alien thoughts ',
it is necessary that the object on which the desire
is directed in the imagination of man should
become as if transparent, so that it may lose its
daemonic power, and set free the looking towards
God. It is different in the dominion of the
natural existence of man, his life with nature, his
work, his friendships, his marriage, his solidarity
with the community ; here the object of the
inclination and the joy should remain in all reality,
for they are truly real and not only possible ; one
should, and one must, truly live with all, but one
shall live with all in holiness, one should hallow
all which one does in one's natural life. No
renunciation is commanded. One eats in holiness,
tastes the taste of food in holiness, and the table
becomes an altar. One works in holiness, and
raises up the sparks which hide themselves in all
tools. One walks in holiness across the fields, and
the soft songs of all herbs, which they voice to God,
enter into the song of our soul. One drinks in
holiness to each other with one's companions, and
it is as if one read together in the Torah. One
dances the roundelay in holiness, and a brightness
shines over the gathering. A husband is united
with his wife in holiness, and the shekhinah rests
over them.

The love between husband and wife is, as is
well-known, a high principle of existence in the
Kabbalah, not only because it offers an image of the
union of ' the sefiroth ' of the emanated spheres,
and also of the decisive union between God and the

shekhinah, but also because it is of utmost importance for the sake of the redemption that the holy
souls who have not yet completed their earthly
wandering are incarnated through conception and
birth, and drawn into the terrestrial world.   Nothing can so well make clear to us the contrast of the
appearances after the sabbatinian crises as when we
set side by side what has developed out of that conception in Frankism and in Chassidism.   I can
here only give one more characteristic example of
each development.

In the chronicle which Frank's disciples wrote
of his deeds, it is told how Frank during his em-
prisonment in Czenstochow, where he enjoyed a
very far-reaching freedom, directed the request
to the women of his circle, called ' the sisters ',
that they should unanimously choose one from
among themselves as a representative of them all,
and hand her over to him ; he would take her to
himself, and she would be blessed through the
birth of a daughter.   His wife, who was with him,
offered that she should be the person chosen, but
he declined her, as it was decided for her that she
should bear sons and not daughters.   As the
rivalries could not be overcome, ' the sisters '
could not reach a unanimous decision, and, after a
violent quarrel, they asked ' the holy lord ' that he
should make the choice himself.   Frank was seized
by a fit of great anger, which lasted for some
weeks.

Over against this grotesque event, whose speci-
fically religious background is, however, unmistakable, I put a small occurrence which I have taken
from the record which a grandson of Rabbi Mordechai of Stachow wrote of his grandfather's life.
At first Rabbi Mordechai was a pupil of Rabbi
Elimelech of Lisensk, and after the latter's death he
became a pupil of ' the Seer ' of Lublin.   The Seer
said once to him : ' We will now hand over to you

a couple of hundred Jews so that you yourself may lead a community '. Rabbi Mordechai answered that he would consult his wife. When he returned home and told her of the proposal, she exclaimed : ' Enough, enough, let us first of all be Jews ourselves '. He then went back to the Lubliner, and declared that he could not accept his suggestion, and gave as his reason what his wife had said. When the Seer heard it, he said : ' From now on do not come to me on the festivals, but remain with your wife. The holy souls wait for you two'.

# NOTES

# NOTES

## The Faith of Judaism

This essay was written in 1928 as a lecture for a School in Political Science to be held at Reichenhall ; it was delivered under the aegis of the Weltwirtschaftlichen Institut of Kiel.

*p. 1.* 1. A religious movement which arose within the Jewry of Eastern Europe towards the middle of the eighteenth century. It derives its name from Hebrew chassid=a pious man. For a further exposition of the teaching of the movement see pp. 89 ff.

*p. 2.* 2. Moses Maimonides (1135–1204) composed his ' Thirteen Principles of Faith ' as part of his commentary on the Mishnah. Apart from the sh'ma these articles constitute the nearest approach of Judaism to a creed. Though they never attained canonical validity and sanction as a creed, they hold an extremely important place in Judaism as the considered statement of one of its foremost teachers. They occur in the Morning Service, see *The Daily Prayer Book*, ed. Singer, pp. 89–90, and are as follows :

1. I believe with perfect faith that the Creator, blessed be his name, is the Author and Guide of everything that has been created, and that he alone has made, does make, and will make all things.

2. I believe with perfect faith that the Creator, blessed be his name, is a Unity, and that there is no unity in any manner like unto his, and that he alone is our God, who was, is, and will be.

3. I believe with perfect faith that the Creator, blessed be his name, is not a body, and that he is free from all the accidents of matter, and that he has not any form whatsoever.

4. I believe with perfect faith that the Creator, blessed be his name, is the first and the last.

5. I believe with perfect faith that to the Creator, blessed be his name, and to him alone, it is right to pray, and that it is not right to pray to any being besides him.

6. I believe with perfect faith that all the words of the prophets are true.

7. I believe with perfect faith that the prophecy of Moses our teacher, peace be unto him, was true, and that he was the chief of the prophets, both of those that preceded and of those that followed him.

8. I believe with perfect faith that the whole Law,

now in our possession, is the same that was given to Moses our teacher, peace be unto him.

9. I believe with perfect faith that this Law will not be changed, and that there will never be any other law from the Creator, blessed be his name.

10. I believe with perfect faith that the Creator, blessed be his name, knows every deed of the children of men, and all their thoughts, as it is said, It is he that fashioneth the hearts of them all, that giveth heed to all their deeds.

11. I believe with perfect faith that the Creator, blessed be his name, rewards those that keep his commandments, and punishes those that transgress them.

12. I believe with perfect faith in the coming of the Messiah, and, though he tarry, I will wait daily for his coming.

13. I believe with perfect faith that there will be a resurrection of the dead at the time when it shall please the Creator, blessed be his name, and exalted be the remembrance of him for ever and ever.

*p. 3.* 3. I have retained the German prefix *ur-* in all those cases where no single, adequate word exists for it in English. In these cases it is used in the same sense as in English philology, into which it has already penetrated, and may be found in combinations like *ur-*Germanic or *ur-*Hamlet, denoting not only the original, primordial, archetypal Germanic, or Hamlet, but also that from which all later manifestations spring, which forms the basis for them, and behind which it is impossible to go.

*p. 4.* 4. The opening words of the sh'ma. This consists in its entirety of *Deut.* 6.4–9, 11.13–21, *Num.* 15.37–41. Its shorter form, *Deut,* 6, 4, is the older form, but both forms date from pre-Christian times. The shorter form is quoted by Jesus in the Gospel according to St Mark, 12.29–30, where Jesus in answer to the Scribe's question as to which is the first commandment of all, says : ' Hear, O Israel, the Lord our God, the Lord is One. And thou shalt love the Lord thy God with all thine heart and with all thy soul, and with all thy might.' For a discussion of this, see I. Abrahams, *Studies in Pharisaism and the Gospels,* First Series, pp. 18–29.

*p. 6.* 5. According to rabbinical teaching man possesses two impulses, ' the evil impulse ' (yetzer ha-ra'), and ' the good impulse ' (yetzer tobh). Both impulses were created by God, and the chief seat of both is in the mind. Thus Judaism regards the moral and mental nature of Adam as unchanged by the Fall. Like the sin of Adam the sins of other human beings are an acquiescence in the suggestions made by one part of man's nature to act in a way contrary to the will of God. The Hebrew word yetzer = impulse, imagination, drive is translated in the A.V. and the R.V. by ' imagination ', while the Hebrew word lebh is translated heart, in spite of the fact that in Hebrew the heart is considered to be the seat of the moral and mental nature of man rather than of his affective nature. The translation of the two words thus tend to obscure to English readers the biblical background for the conception of the two yetzers.

*p. 8.* 6. The Mishnah embodies the Oral Law of Judaism as this has developed during the four centuries 200 B.C.-200 A.D., and was codified by Rabbi Judah the Prince towards the end of the second century A.D. ' " The Law " (*Torah*), which it was the Mishnah's purpose to cherish and develop, is a complex conception. It includes the Written Law, the laws explicitly recorded in the Five Books of Moses ; it includes also " the tradition of the elders " of the Oral Law, namely, such beliefs and religious practices as piety and custom had in the course of centuries, consciously or unconsciously, grafted on to or developed out of the Written Law ; and it included yet a third, less tangible element, a spirit of development, whereby Written Law and Oral Law, in spite of seeming differences, are brought into a unity and interpreted and re-interpreted to meet the needs of changed conditions ' (Herbert Danby, *The Mishnah. Translated from the Hebrew*, pp. xiii–xiv).

*p. 8.* 7. Mishnah, *Yoma*, 8.9. The passage reads, in Danby's translation : ' R. Akiba said : Blessed are ye, O Israel, Before whom are ye made clean and who makes you clean ? Your Father in heaven ; as it is written, *And I will sprinkle clean water upon you and ye shall be clean* (*Ezekiel*, 36.25). And again it says, *O Lord the hope* (mikweh) *of Israel* (*Jeremiah*, 17.13) ; as the *Mikweh* cleanses the unclean so does the Holy One, blessed be he, cleanse Israel.' In his exegesis R. Akiba plays upon the double meaning of *mikweh*, which is used for both ' hope ' and ' immersion-pool '.

*p. 9.* 8. Shekhinah may roughly be translated by ' presence of God '. It denotes both God as present in the world and as seen or felt by human beings. A great deal has been written on the material manifestations of the shekhinah, as light, as a cloud, as a soughing, rustling movement, and again on the shekhinah as personified. See *i.a.* J. Abelson, *The Immanence of God in Rabbinical Literature*. The following commentary on *Exodus*, 40.35 gives the famous illustration of the omnipresence of the shekhinah :

' It is written, " And Moses was not able to enter into the tent of meeting, because the glory of the Lord filled the sanctuary ". R. Joshua of Sikhnin said in the name of R. Levi : The matter is like a cave which lies by the sea shore : the tide rises, and the cave becomes full of water, but the sea is no whit less full. So the sanctuary and the tent of meeting were filled with the radiance of the Shechinah, but the world was no less filled with God's glory ' (Num. R., Naso XII, 4. Quoted from Montefiore and Loewe, *A Rabbinic Anthology*, no. 27).

*p. 11.* 9. See note 6 *supra*. Torah is usually translated ' Law ', a translation which is as inadequate and misleading as it is well-established. Torah is a revelation of religion, it is both the means of revelation and the content of that revelation ; a somewhat more adequate translation would therefore be ' teaching ', ' instruction ', ' religion '. Torah includes ' all that God has made known of his nature, character, and purpose, and of what he would have man be and do '. Further, Torah is inexhaustible, a conception which gives to Judaism its capacity for development. See G. Foote Moore, *Judaism*, i. 248, 263-67.

*p. 12.* 10. The Talmud consists of the Mishnah and its commentary, the Gemara (=completion). There are two Talmuds, one, the Palestinian or Jerusalem Talmud, which was compiled in Palestine between the end of the second century and the middle of the fifth century ; and one, the Babylonian Talmud, which was compiled in Mesopotamia between the middle of the fourth century and the beginning of the sixth century. Neither Talmud was compiled in order to fix and stabilise the teaching, but in order to make it available for study. A good conception of the content of the Talmud may be obtained from Dr. A. Cohen's small volume, *Everyman's Talmud* (J. M. Dent & Sons, 1932).

*p. 13.* 11. Kabbalah. This is a vast esoteric system, half magical, half philosophic, wholly emanational ; the apocryphal books of *Enoch* and *Jubilees*, as well as the visions of Ezekiel, play an important part in it. It is often bizarre, fantastic, grotesque in its speculations on cosmology and cosmogony, but it also contains pure mystical teaching of a very high level.

### The Two Centres of the Jewish Soul

An address delivered to the Conference of the Four Societies for Mission to the Jews in the German Language, held at Stuttgart in March, 1930.

*p. 25.* 1. Gojim, plural of goj = non-Jew.

*p. 26.* 2. Tannaites, a comprehensive name for the Palestinian rabbis of 10 A.D.–220 A.D. The Tannaites are divided into six generations of varying lengths, each generation being represented by one ' pair ' of distinguished scholars. Thus Tannaitic I, 10–80, is represented by Johanan ben Zakkai, who founded the Academy of Jamnia after the Destruction of Jerusalem, and Gamaliel I, known from *Acts*, 5.34. The greatest rabbi of Tannaitic V, 165–200, is Rabbi Judah the Prince, who codified the Mishnah. The Mishnah is the work of the Tannaites.

*p. 28.* 3. haggadic, adj. of haggadah. The content of the Talmud is divided into halakhah and haggadah. Halakhah, literally ' walking ' or ' way ', hence ' custom ' is the exposition and application of the legal elements in Scripture ; haggadah, literally ' narration ', is the elaboration and development of the historical, moral, and religious elements in Scripture for didactic purposes.

## *Imitatio Dei*

The author originally contemplated making this essay a part of a larger work ; it is therefore furnished with a series of notes and references which I give below, marked (a).

*p. 31.* 1. 176B–D. (a)
*p. 31.* 2. Stobaeus, *Eclogae* ed. Wachsmuth, ii 249, 8. (a)
*p. 31.* 3. Iamblichus, *Vitae Pythagorae*, 137. (a)
*p. 31.* 4. 248A. (a)
*p. 32.* 5. V. 11. (a)
*p. 32.* 6. Strabo, viii 353. (a)
*p. 32.* 7. 1. 527. (a)
*p. 32.* 8. *e.g.* 1, 580 ; 14, 276 ; 15, 18 (a)
*p. 33.* 9. Frg. 70. (a)
*p. 33.* 10. The Trojan Women, 884. (a)
*p. 33.* 11. 5, 1. (a)
*p. 33.* 12. 14, 9. (a)
*p. 34.* 13. 8, 2. (a)
*p. 34.* 14. Irenaeus in Eusebius, *History of the Church*, v. 20. (a)
*p. 34.* 15. Martyrium Polycarpi, 1, 2. (a)
*p. 34.* 16. Eusebius, IV, 15. (a)
*p. 35.* 17. Ubertinus de Casali, Arbor vitae crucifixae (1312). (a)
*p. 36.* 18. Laws, 636D. (a)
*p. 36.* 19. 7, 2. (a)
*p. 36.* 20. I, 11.1. (a)

*p. 37.* 21. Midrash. Moral and religious teaching given in the synagogues and collected to form one branch of rabbinic literature. The sayings and teaching of well-known rabbis were written down and copied from one midrashic collection to another, sometimes under the rabbi's name, sometimes not. The earliest collection we possess dates from the fourth century A.D., but contains much older material. The most important collection of midrashim is the *Midrash Rabbah*, or the Great Midrash, which forms a commentary on the Pentateuch, and Song of Songs, Ruth, Lamentations, Ecclesiastes, Esther. The illustration given in note 1 to page 12 is from this Midrash collection. The final form of the midrash dates from the twelfth century, but the main content is from the talmudic period.

*p. 37.* 22. Debarim Rabba *passim.* (a)

*p. 37.* 23. Pesikta Rabbáti, ed. Friedmann, 46b. (a)

*p. 38.* 24. After the קרי should be read לא, and not לו. (a)

*p. 38.* 25. Bereschit Rabba on 49, 29. (a)

*p. 39.* 26. Sayings of the Fathers, iii. (a). This forms the ninth section of the fourth division of the Mishnah. It may conveniently be found in *The Daily Prayer Book*, ed. Singer, pp. 184–209e.

*p. 39.* 27. Jalkut Reubeni on I.M. 1, 27 in the name of ספר החיים. For the distinction between 'image' and 'likeness' see *Midrasch Tanchuma*, ed. S. Buber, 15. (a).

*p. 39.* 28. באר מיים חיים. on I.M. 1, 26 (Warsaw edition, p. 39). (a)

*p. 39.* 29. Mid. Schochar tob on Ps. 1. 1. (a)

*p. 40.* 30. mizwah, literally, ' commandment ', thence ' precept ', thence ' charity ' ; used of any specific duty of man to his neighbour ; a charitable, friendly, or religious deed to one's fellow-man.

*p. 40.* 31. Sifra on III.M. 19, 2. Cp. Lewy, ' Über eine Fragmente aus der Mischna des Abba Saul ', 23, *Anm.* 53. (a)

*p. 41.* 32. The saying of Abba Schaul's is surely given most correctly in Jeruschalmi Pea 15b, the readings of Babli, Schabbat 133b and Mechilta 37a are obviously corrupt. Cp. for the textual emendation Bacher, ' Die Agada der Tannaiten ii,' 367, *Anm.* 2, and also Abrahams *Studies in Pharisaism*, ii, 175 (in the inspiring essay ' The Imitation of God ') ; Abrahams, however, does not take the correct read-

ing into consideration ; see also, Marmorstein, ' Die Nachahmung Gottes in der Agada ' in *Jeschurun*, xiv (1927), 622f. (a)

*p. 41.* 33. French commentator on the Bible and
Talmud. Born in Troyes 1040, died 1105.

*p. 41.* 34. To the passage quoted in Babli. (a)

*p. 41.* 35. The possible connection between this interpretation and the secret name אני והו with which God was
called upon during the procession round the altar at the Feast
of Tabernacles (Mischnah, Sukka IV, 5) cannot be discussed
here. Cp. Klein, *Der alteste christliche Katechismus*, 44ff ;
see also M. Buber, *Konigtum Gottes*, 215f., and Marmorstein,
*The Old Rabbinic Doctrine of God*, 84. (a)

*p. 41.* 36. Sifre on V.M. 11,22 and Sota 14a. (a)

*p. 41.* 37. Schechter, Aspects of Rabbinic Theology,
119. (a)

*p. 41.* 38. For the expression הלך אחרי אלהים. may be
compared the article by Gulin, ' Die Nachfolge Gottes ',
which, however, does not do justice to the essentially religious
meaning of the words. (a)

*p. 41.* 39. middoth, literally ' norms ', then the norms
of God's dealing with men, *e.g.* merciful and righteous, then
attribute of God. (Studia Orientalia I., Helsingfors 1925,
34ff).

*p. 42.* 40. Bereschit Rabba on I.M., 23, 19. (a)

*p. 42.* 41. Cp. also Marmorstein, *Die Nachahmung
Gottes*, 624ff. (a)

## Biblical Leadership

Given as a lecture in Munich, 1928.

*p. 54.* 1. A literal translation of the biblical term as
used by the author.

## Trust

This short essay was written as early as 1926, and does not,
as one might be inclined to think, date from the rise of
Nazism.

## Spirit and Body in the Chassidic Movement

*p. 77.* 1. zaddik, literally ' a righteous man ' ; used
specially of the head of a chassidic community.

*p. 78.* 2. gelilah, ' the act of rolling up ' the wrappings
of the Law in its vestments after the lesson has been read

from it.    For a further discussion of this, see Jewish Encyclopedia *sub voce*.

*p. 85.*    3.    kawanoth, plural of kawanah, the concentration and intention of prayer ;   in the plural form used of meditations and thence of the words guiding the meditation.

*p. 88.*    4.    This is a succinct description of what is known in Christian mysticism as the ligature.

*p. 88.*    5.    minchah, the afternoon service of the synagogue.